Teacher Preparation Classroom

See a
www.prenhall.com

Your Class. Their Careers. Our Future. Will your students be prepared?

We invite you to explore our new, innovative and engaging website and all that it has to offer you, your course, and tomorrow's educators! Preview this site today at www.prenhall.com/teacherprep/demo. Just click on "go" on the login page to begin your exploration.

Organized around the major courses pre-service teachers take, the Teacher Preparation site provides media, student/teacher artifacts, strategies, research articles, and other resources to equip your students with the quality tools needed to excel in their courses and prepare them for their first classroom.

This ultimate online education resource will provide you and your students access to:

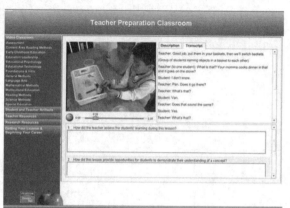

Online Video Library. More than 250 video clips—each tied to a course topic and framed by learning goals and Praxis-type questions—capture real teachers and students working in real classrooms.

Student and Teacher Artifacts. More than 200 student and teacher classroom artifacts—each tied to a course topic and framed by learning goals and application questions—provide a wealth of materials and experiences to help your students observe children's developmental learning.

Lesson Plan Builder. Step-by-step guidelines and lesson plan examples support students as they learn to build high-quality lesson plans.

Articles and Readings. Over 500 articles from ASCD's renowned journal *Educational Leadership* are available. The site also includes Research Navigator, a searchable database of additional educational journals.

Strategies and Lessons. Over 500 research-supported instructional strategies appropriate for a wide range of grade levels and content areas.

Licensure and Career Tools. Resources devoted to helping your students pass their licensure exam; learn standards, law, and public policies; plan a teaching portfolio; and succeed in their first year of teaching.

How to ORDER *Teacher Prep* for you and your students:

For students to receive a *Teacher Prep* Access Code with this text, instructors **must** provide a special value pack ISBN number on their textbook order form. To receive this special ISBN, please email **Merrill.marketing@pearsoned.com** and provide the following information:
- Name and Affiliation
- Author/Title/Edition of Merrill text

Upon ordering *Teacher Prep* for their students, instructors will be given a lifetime *Teacher Prep* Access Code.

Teaching English Learners and Immigrant Students in Secondary Schools

Christian J. Faltis and Cathy A. Coulter
Arizona State University

PEARSON
Merrill
Prentice Hall

Upper Saddle River, New Jersey
Columbus, Ohio

Library of Congress Cataloging-in-Publication Data

Faltis, Christian
   Teaching English learners and immigrant students in secondary school / Christian J. Faltis and Cathy A. Coulter.
       p.   cm.
   Includes bibliographical references.
   ISBN 0-13-119241-8 (pbk. : alk. paper)   1. English language—Study and teaching (Secondary)—Foreign speakers.
2. English language—Study and teaching (Secondary)—United States.   3. Immigrants—Education—United States.
4. Education, Bilingual—United States.   I. Coulter, Cathy.   II. Title.
   PE1128.A2F25 2008
   428.2'4—dc22

                                                                                            2006036373

Vice President and Executive Publisher: Jeffery W. Johnston
Executive Editor: Debra A. Stollenwerk
Production Editor: Alexandrina Benedicto Wolf
Production Coordination: GGS Book Services
Design Coordinator: Diane C. Lorenzo
Cover Designer: Janna Thompson-Chordas
Cover Image: Jupiter Images
Photo Coordinator: Maria B. Vonada
Production Manager: Susan W. Hannahs
Director of Marketing: David Gesell
Senior Marketing Manager: Darcy Betts Prybella
Marketing Coordinator: Brian Mounts

This book was set in New Baskerville by UG/GGS Information Services. It was printed and bound by R.R. Donnelley & Sons Company. The cover was printed by R.R. Donnelley & Sons Company.

Pearson Education Ltd.
Pearson Education Singapore, Pte. Ltd.
Pearson Education Canada, Ltd.
Pearson Education–Japan.

Pearson Education Australia Pty Limited
Pearson Education North Asia Ltd.
Pearson Educación de Mexico, S.A. de C.V.
Pearson Education Malaysia Pte. Ltd.

10 9 8 7 6 5 4 3 2 1
ISBN-13: 978-0-13-119241-6
ISBN-10:   0-13-119241-8

Preface

Teaching English Learners and Immigrant Students in Secondary Schools is a college-level textbook written for preservice and practicing teachers at the secondary level. In this book, we provide foundational knowledge about the legal, historical, and current rationales for educating students for whom English learning is an additional language. We rely on the sociocultural theories regarding teaching and learning for adolescent English learners, the fastest growing group of secondary students nationwide.

This book combines the elements necessary in preservice and inservice classes for secondary teachers. It includes four content-based chapters on language arts, science, math, and social studies that are practical guides for classes populated by English learners from various academic and language backgrounds. Many students who enter secondary school are immigrants with variable formal schooling and literacy experiences. We offer suggestions on how to address the needs of newcomer immigrant students (arriving within the last 3–5 years) and students with low first language literacy abilities. Throughout the book, we continue to suggest ways to include this population of immigrant English learners in your teaching and learning plans.

This book does not pretend to prepare secondary teachers to teach English as a second language. That is a different field of study, which requires extensive coursework in linguistics, applied linguistics, and language teaching methodology. Rather, the main focus of this book is the preparing of secondary content area teachers who will have English learners and immigrant students in their classes. This book provides a wide variety of effective approaches and strategies to help English learners and immigrant students succeed in school.

THEORETICAL/CONCEPTUAL FRAMEWORK

Teaching English Learners and Immigrant Students in Secondary Schools is based on sociocultural learning theories. From these theoretical perspectives, we offer readers five commitments in practice to facilitate the success of English learners in all classrooms, including mainstream classrooms. Our commitments in practice are based on the premise that learners are apprenticed into academic communities of practice (both real and imagined). We believe that learners will choose to participate in learning when activities are challenging, interesting, and culturally relevant. In Chapter 2 we provide a full definition of academic communities of practice to show that students who are invited into these classrooms, and whose interactions around academic content and language are supported through a variety of meaningful scaffolds, will experience academic success. We show how new immigrant English learners can gain access to the discursive properties and norms of interaction within content-based classroom communities by gaining academic identities without being forced to let go of their unique sociocultural identities. Further, we show and discuss ways for students to become active citizens for social justice by expanding what they learn in class to their surrounding local communities.

We believe that all students benefit from a diverse classroom, and this book shows how teachers can organize and structure classroom practices to ensure the inclusion, contribution, and academic success of all students, especially those English language learners. The teaching approaches and theories in which they are based are all contextualized within historical and current perceptions and laws on how to teach secondary English learners, including newcomer immigrant students with little or no experience communicating in English.

We make no bones about being advocates for adolescent English learners and immigrant students, regardless of the their legal status or prior formal schooling experiences. The Supreme Court has made it clear from its ruling in *Plyler v. Doe* (1982) that all children residing in the United States have the right to a free public education without regard to their own or their parent's immigration status. As the judge in the case against a Texas statute that sought to deny access to public schools to children and youth of illegal immigrants pointed out, the Texas law "imposes a lifetime hardship on a discrete class of children not accountable for their disabling status" (*Plyler v. Doe*, 1982, p. 219). We take the stance that we, as educators, must do all we can to provide immigrant students and English learners the opportunity to learn English and become educated in math, science, literature, the arts, and social studies; to do anything less is exclusionary and unacceptable in a democratic society.

We are excited about what this text can bring to classroom instruction and discussions in preservice and inservice classes and beyond, and we hope readers will share this excitement and advocacy as they become increasingly aware of what it takes to be successful teachers of English learners at all levels of English proficiency.

ORGANIZATION OF THE TEXT

This book includes three main sections with nine chapters. In Section I, Chapter 1 lays out the historical, legal, and educational rationale for the kinds of commitments in practice that we advocate for teaching secondary English learners. Chapter 2 presents a discussion of the theoretical principles of teaching and learning for young adults and adolescents. It explores the theory that drives the approaches to teaching and learning we promote. Chapter 3 describes current programs, including Newcomer Centers, that meet the needs of recently arriving immigrant students.

Section II, Chapters 4 through 7, represents the *sine qua non* of this book; it is through these chapters that readers learn how teachers who are successful with English learners realize the commitments in practice for their particular content area. Each chapter opens with a classroom scenario in which immigrant students are actively participating as they learn English and are acquired into the academic community of practice aligned with particular academic content. Specific content areas included are language arts, math (geometry), social studies (history), and science (physics). Practicing teachers contributed to the development of the chapters on math and science. Diane Whitmore of Phoenix, Arizona, shared her ideas. John Morrison of Clarkston, Michigan, contributed activities for the physics chapter (Chapter 7). The other two chapters are a result of our work in secondary schools with language arts and social studies teachers. We used vignettes in three chapters because we believe that readers will make better sense of the strategies we present if they are embedded in real classroom activities. To be successful with English learners, secondary teachers need commitments in practice, which include strategies for facilitating equitable participation, discussion, understanding, and ultimately learning. Some of the practices we champion in the scenarios will be familiar; others will be new. The goal is that readers will be able to see how effective teachers engage in practices that support their commitments in practice.

In Section III, Chapter 8 presents an overview of issues and practices regarding assessment. We believe that there are important roles for assessment in secondary school and for English learners. Clearly, teachers need to use assessment to help guide instructional decisions. Assessment is also valuable for making decisions about special English language support for English learners. Lastly, for students who intend to pursue higher education, learning how to take tests, such as the SAT or ACT, is imperative. Nonetheless, there are many ways that assessment has become abusive and intrusive to teachers and students alike. In this chapter, we suggest ways for teachers to incorporate authentic assessment practices and to question testing practices used on English learners.

The Afterword is organized around the idea that for English learners and immigrants to have successful experiences in school from the outset, teachers, counselors, support staff, and peers need to see these students as capable learners. Here we present a rationale for inviting immigrant students and English learners into the school community, arguing that how these students are defined initially contributes greatly to how well they will be accepted and accept new identities as academic learners in school-based communities of practice.

FEATURES OF THE TEXT

This book is unique in that it provides all of the foundational, theoretical, and methodological features that will prepare classroom teachers to provide effective instruction for English learners.

In addition, *Teaching English Learners and Immigrant Students in Secondary Schools* provides the following special features:

- *Commitments in Practice:* Five principles that reflect commitments in practice to guide effective teaching and learning for immigrant English learners.

- *Historical Overview:* An historical overview of the inception of high schools and how their beginnings have influenced their current structure.

- *Current, State-of-the-Art Learning Theories:* Approaches and strategies we advocate and present are based on recent sociocultural teaching and learning theories.

- *Chapter Overview/Vignettes:* The first three chapters begin with an overview that helps guide the reader. Chapter 4 provides specific reference to the commitments in practice within the language arts to help readers visualize how various content area teachers can enable immigrant English learners to learn academic content as they are learning English. We leave it up to the readers in discussion circles to exchange ideas about where and how the commitments in practice show up in subsequent content chapters.

- *Within-Chapter Reflections:* Questions for reflection are included in several chapters to encourage readers to reflect on the chapter's information.

- *End-of-Chapter Activities:* For the content area chapters, we have included questions and activities at the end of the chapter to encourage readers to relate what they learned to their own circumstances as preservice and inservice teachers.

- *Chapter Summaries:* For each chapter, we provide summaries of the key points that are covered in the chapter and that readers should understand, know, and if appropriate, use in their own classroom settings.

TO THE TEACHER

This book is organized to give your students an understanding of the historical and legal rationales for bilingual schooling practices before introducing them to theoretical underpinnings of the teaching and learning practices we present as commitments in practice. We provide classroom scenarios that include many examples to draw from, but undoubtedly you will want to bring in your own experiences and examples to fit your particular circumstances and your areas of interest and expertise. You may wish to begin your class with a particular content area theme, and then as you move students into the later chapters, which address different content areas, compare that theme with new content areas. We suggest that your students spend some time talking with teachers who are working in multilingual classrooms to learn about their experiences and compare what they learn from the teachers to the ideas and strategies we present in the book.

It is important to stress to your students that this book is not a recipe of adjustments or strategies for teaching adolescent English learners. We want readers to understand teaching as commitments in practice that guide their decisions about how to best serve the needs of immigrant students and English learners. Finally, you will need to continually stress to your students that it takes time to become proficient in English, especially in the registers of English required to show membership in academic communities of practice. It is not common for English learners who enter secondary school with minimal proficiency in English to become academically fluent within a year's time. On average, most English learners take between 4 and 7 years to become fluent, depending on their prior formal schooling (L1 literacy) experiences, the kinds of English-as-a-second-language coursework they receive, and how prepared their content area teachers are for meeting their language and learning needs (Hakuta, Butler, & Witt, 2000; Prey & MacSwan, 2002; Thomas & Collier, 1997).

TO THE STUDENT

You are the new generation of secondary teachers. Chances are great that many of the students you teach will not be anything like the students who attended your high school. You will be responsible for educating a diverse group of young adults, many of whom are recent immigrants and children of immigrants who are adding English as an additional language as they are learning academic content in your classroom. This book is an introduction to teaching English learners (immigrants and children of immigrants alike) in secondary school for secondary content area teachers. We wrote this book for you, regardless of whether you will be teaching algebra, English literature, biology, psychology, or American history. We are aware that each academic content area has specialized vocabulary, unique histories, and particular ways of communicating ideas. These are for you to master. But in addition to these areas, you also need to know about how to teach immigrant English learners. You will continue to be content area teachers—math teachers, science teachers, history teachers, and English teachers. And you will be teachers of English learners and immigrant students as well.

By reading about, discussing, and trying out the practices and activities we present in this book, we hope you will develop commitments in your practice so that you can become successful with immigrant English learners. You should not be fearful of entering a classroom where some or many of your students are immigrants and English language learners. When you complete this book, and the course in which you use it, you should feel confident that you will be better prepared to teach what you love and share your knowledge with students, regardless of their English language and formal schooling experiences.

REFERENCES

Hakuta, K., Butler, Y., & Witt, D. (2000). *How long does it take English learners to attain proficiency?* Santa Barbara, CA: University of California Linguistic Minority Research Institute.

Plyler v. Doe. (1982). 457 U.S. 202, 102 Supreme Court 2382.

Pray, L., & MacSwan, J. (2002). *Different question, same answer: How long does it take for English learners to attain proficiency?* Paper presented at the annual meeting of the American Educational Research Association, New Orleans, LA.

Thomas, W., & Collier, V. (1997). *School effectiveness for language minority students.* Washington, DC: National Clearinghouse for Bilingual Education.

ACKNOWLEDGEMENTS

We wish to thank and acknowledge Debbie Stollenwerk for supporting this book. We introduced the idea for this book to Debbie nearly 10 years ago, and at that time, there was very little in the way of research or writings about bilingual education or working with adolescent English learners at the secondary school level. When we approached Debbie again, she was excited about doing the book. She has been a wonderful editor to work with, and for that we are truly grateful.

We want to thank the reviewers who provided very helpful suggestions on how to improve the book: Rosie Arenas, California State University—Fresno; Burcu Ates, Texas A&M University; Mary Carol Combs, The University of Arizona; Salvador A. Gabaldón, Tucson Unified School District; Meleidis Gort, University of Miami; Craig A. Hughes, Central Washington University; Ana H. Macias, University of Texas—El Paso; Kip Tellez, University of California Santa Cruz; Paula Wolfe, Mexico State University; and Youngjoo Yi, The University of Alabama. We have tried to include all of their suggestions to the extent that we were able.

Table of Contents

Chapter 5 Teaching and Learning Math for English Learners

I

Historical, Legal, and Educational Rationales

1

Foundations of Teaching English Learners and Immigrant Students in Secondary School

Anthony Magnacca/Merrill

OVERVIEW

This chapter provides you with a historical, legal, and educational rationale for the kinds of commitments in practice that we advocate for teaching adolescent English learners, immigrants and children of immigrants alike, at the secondary level. The guiding questions for this chapter are:

- What were some of the original purposes of high school with respect to educating students to participate in American society?
- What are some of the differences between how immigrants were treated in early high schools and high schools of the present era?
- What are some of the legal foundations regarding the education of English learners?
- What kinds of practices and support do exemplary high schools provide for English learners?
- What happens in schools that underserve the needs of adolescent English learners?

Upon completing this first chapter, you should be able to engage in lengthy and lively discussions about the foundations of education for secondary English learners and begin to understand the gravity of the academic needs of these students. Our stance is that all students, regardless of their language proficiency, immigration history, or past educational experiences, have the right to the best possible education you can provide. This means that, in addition to knowing how to teach your content area specialization, you also need to know how to invite immigrant students who are learning English into your classroom activities, so that they can participate equitably as members of the academic and social practices used for making meaning, for learning academic language, and for learning the content of your class. This chapter provides an overview of the conditions many English learners experience, so that when you make commitment in practice (see Chapter 2) you know the challenges you face and what you can do to overcome them.

All of you have been in high school, but is it likely that most of you have not had engaging experiences with immigrant English learners. In high school, as you well remember, in addition to the group names used to stereotype classmates, students self-segregate into various identity groupings, some ethnic, some having to do with dress and affinities: sports jocks, computer geeks, skaters, band nerds, internationals, *cholo/as*, Mexicans, thugs, vamps, rappers, cowboys/cowgirls, druggies, gothics, and the like. Depending on the groups to which you belonged, how you were identified, and how people identified you, it was quite possible that interaction with classmates outside those groups was minimal, unless they were in the same classes that you took. Moreover, if your classmates spoke a language other than English, and were learning English, you may have gone all the way through high school without exchanging more than a handful of words with these students. We believe that if you learn to incorporate the commitments in practice presented in this book, you will be a better secondary teacher because you will reach students who historically as well as currently have been underserved at best, and more often than not, swept under the educational rug. We begin this journey by examining the purpose of early American high schools, and then move on to some of the legal battles fought to ensure that the high schools of today provide English learners with equitable educational opportunities to participate in and benefit from learning in your classrooms.

EARLY AMERICAN HIGH SCHOOLS

High schools began springing up mainly across the more populated midwestern and eastern states during the latter half of the 19th century, in an era of ambiguity and change. Once the idea of schools that gave students the opportunity to study academic subjects beyond the 8th grade gained popularity, enrollment soared, especially for second- and third-generation children of the developing middle classes. However, what exactly high school was meant to accomplish for these students became the focus of heated debates in the early 20th century. The debates centered on how high schools should be organized and what curriculum should be offered, especially in light of the new waves of poorer, darker, less educated immigrants from eastern and southern Europe that began to inundate the country at the turn of the century.

Some supporters of the new public high school argued for a comprehensive education open to all students (except African Americans, Native Americans, and Mexican Americans) and distinct from the college preparation curriculum private academies provided for college-bound students, most of whom were the children of the elite class (Tyack, 1974). Others argued that the high school should be modeled after the European dual structure, with certain schools for college-bound students and others for students interested in preparing for vocations.

THE CARDINAL PRINCIPLES OF SECONDARY EDUCATION

While the debate continued, in 1918 the Bureau of Education under the direction of the Department of the Interior issued a publication in support of a comprehensive high school. The publication was titled the *Cardinal Principles of Secondary Education*, Bulletin No. 35, and its purpose was to establish that American public high schools were to be framed to achieve two primary functions:

1. To provide a comprehensive educational curriculum which enables students to study in more depth specialized areas of history, mathematics, science, and English; and
2. To unify students of diverse background, abilities, and aspirations (Wraga, 1994).

Although consensus over merits of a comprehensive high school for all students continued to be disputed, educators and political leaders alike unanimously endorsed the second function, that of developing and maintaining the language and cultural dominance of White, Anglo Saxons.

Coming at the heels of World War I, and coupled with increased immigration from eastern and southern Europe, the new educational policy on unification reflected a widespread fear that was based on the conviction that America at the turn of the century was becoming too diverse and overly populated by non-White immigrants. This fear stoked the flames of Americanization efforts, which viewed any attempt by new immigrants to retain cultural traditions and behaviors or to maintain languages other than English while residing in the United States as un-American and a threat to the dominant American cultural model. The words of President Teddy Roosevelt, who in 1917 gave the following speech, make this perspective abundantly clear:

> We must have one flag. We must also have but one language. That must be the language of the Declaration of Independence, of Washington's farewell address, of Lincoln's Gettysburg speech and second inaugural. We cannot tolerate any attempt to oppose or supplant the language and culture that has come down to us from the builders of this Republic. (Flores & Murrillo, 2001, p. 194)

Accordingly, the *Cardinal Principles of Secondary Education* served notice to high schools that one of their main functions was to "unify" students by making sure they learned the language and culture of those in power and of those who colonized the United States first, in other words, the "we."

Americanization was acceptable among descendants of the "builders of the Republic" because a few prominent White scientists, anthropologists, and educators at the turn of the century were eager to promote their racist belief that new immigrants, especially those of color, were genetically and culturally inferior to the original White, Anglo-Saxon colonial immigrants. Tyack (1974) summarizes these efforts:

> Bogus anthropologists divided the peoples of Europe into "races" and popularizers were quick to brand the "Teuton" or "Nordic" race superior to the "Alpine," "Mediterranean," and Jewish breeds. Immigration during the three decades before World War I consisted largely of people from southern and eastern Europe. These "new immigrants" were "illiterate, docile, lacking in self-reliance and initiative, and not possessing the Anglo-Saxon conceptions of law, order, and government," the educator Ellwood Cubberley complained in 1909. "Their coming has served to dilute tremendously our national stock, and to corrupt our national life." Cubberley believed that the only way was to break up the ghettoes, for the nation was "afflicted with a serious case of racial indigestion." (p. 233)

Because the new immigrants were perceived as a threat to the dominant Anglo-Saxon culture, schools sought to indoctrinate immigrant children by enjoining them to pledge their allegiance to the United States. At one school in New York during World War II, the school day started like this:

> First thing in the morning . . . is the salute to the flag and the singing of the Star Spangled Banner. This is no post–Pearl Harbor patriotism. It has always been the procedure from time immemorial . . . An American flag hangs in every classroom and from the first day the children enter school they are taught to revere the flag and to love America. This was so when their fathers went to school and when their grandfathers went to school and it is still so. They begin to study American history from the moment they know how to read. The first stories are about America's heroes, Washington, Jefferson, Lincoln. . . . (Cuban, 1993, p. 230)

In addition to Americanizing immigrant children, high schools, in particular, became places where students were tracked into various kinds of specializations, depending on their social, economic, and immigrant status. Students from poorer socioeconomic backgrounds (which included most new immigrants) were restricted to basic coursework and vocational tracks, whereas the children of the more privileged society were tracked into the more serious college preparation classes. Oddly enough, school reformers in the early 20th century were convinced that schools could improve the lot of new immigrants by addressing their perceived mental deficiencies and developing a new

■ **Reflection**

High schools play a substantial role in shaping society. Do you think high schools should strive to build a society based on one culture or a society in which many cultures coexist?

cadre of workers for the manual trades, which would provide support for the more skillful and powerful careers of the privileged classes.

So it was that the dual functions of high schools for unification and specialization played out in the lives of immigrant children. Immigrants were to become Americans, abandoning any and all affinities toward old customs, traditions, and ways of using language. In school, new immigrants were tracked into coursework that would prepare them for their place in a stratified society: patriotic citizens who were to embrace their role in this new country, that of a working underclass.

HIGH SCHOOLS AND IMMIGRATION IN THE PRESENT ERA

In many ways, high schools in the present era have changed little from their inception as sites for stratifying and developing patriotic adolescent youth. Students continue to be tracked into different academic level courses, and the curriculum offered is geared toward ensuring the preservation of Anglo-centric history, literature, and cultural tradition. Structurally and organizationally, as well, high schools today are almost indistinguishable from high schools of 50 and 75 years ago. In the modern buildings of today, adolescents between the ages of 14 and 19 change classes in hallways; congregate by group, class, and gender affinities; study curriculum stratified into levels or tracks; and many engage in school sports and other extracurricular activities. School spirit is encouraged through school colors, a mascot to represent sports teams and the student body, and pep rallies geared to generate a public expression of school affiliation. Classes are taught in 55-minute blocks or longer, and students are required to complete a certain number of Carnegie units to graduate within a time frame of 4 years.

Similar to the turn of the last century, high schools today are populated with a burgeoning number of new immigrant students who speak languages other than English and who arrive in school with a range of formal schooling experiences. With the exception of Native American peoples, all residents of the United States are either immigrants or children of immigrants. The new immigrants of the present era share some commonalities with the transoceanic experiences of immigrants in the early 20th century. Both groups of immigrants migrated to the United States to improve their social and economic conditions; to escape ethnic, religious, and political persecution; or to join their families and loved ones who are already here.

Despite these similarities, much has changed since the early beginnings of high schools. Up until the 1950s and as late as the 1970s, there were separate, segregated high schools for White students and students of color; namely, African American, American Indian, and Mexican students. In 1954, the Supreme Court ruled in *Brown v. Board of Education* that the segregation of children of color from White students was discriminatory, because segregated schools meant that children of color experienced educational opportunities that were inferior to those of children in White schools. Accordingly, the Supreme Court ordered the integration of all public schools in the United States and outlawed separate public schools for Whites and children of color. Initially, *Brown v. Board of Education* was aimed at desegregating schools for African American and White students, but its effect was eventually extended to Indian boarding schools and schools for Mexican-origin children in the Southwest.

Subsequent federal policy concerning the education of non-English-speaking immigrant students and children of immigrants began to surface in the mid-1960s with the passage of the Civil Rights Act (1964), which broadly banned discrimination on the basis of race, color, or national origin in any federally assisted program (meaning public schools) (Ovando, Collier, & Combs, 2003).

BILINGUAL EDUCATION AND THE LAW

Social and Political Events

In the late 1960s and early 1970s, bilingual education, defined as teaching students in their native language while they learned enough English to fully participate in English-only classrooms, became a viable educational option for schools with large numbers of immigrant non-English-speaking students. The introduction of bilingual education was fueled by a number of social and political events that began to surface around the mid-1960s (Judd, 1978, in August & García, 1988). First, bilingual education had been effective in Dade County with Cuban refugee children who settled in South Florida. Second, research conducted in the early and mid-1960s reported that high levels of bilingualism lead to gains in intelligence factors associated with academic achievement (Lambert & Peal, 1962; Jacobs & Pierce, 1966). Third, bolstered by the Civil Rights movement, there was a strong national shift toward cultural pluralism accompanied by ethnic revitalization, notably within Spanish-speaking and bilingual Latino communities. Fourth, President Lyndon Johnson believed strongly that the way to win the War on Poverty was through increasing educational spending on programs geared toward improving education for the nation's poor, which included many immigrants and children of immigrants. Fifth, the Elementary and Secondary Education Act of 1965 had already paved the way for federal intervention in schooling efforts targeted for poor, low-achieving students. Sixth, to combat the spread of communism from Cuba, the United States stepped up its involvement in Central and South America, resulting in the need for increased numbers of Spanish-English bilingual government employees. Seventh, a renewed interest in foreign-language instruction developed as a result of the launching of *Sputnik*. Eighth, the 1960 census data indicated that the Spanish-surnamed population had increased by more than 50%—from 2.3 million in 1950 to nearly 3.5 million in 1960. The data also indicated that Spanish-speaking children were faring poorly in all levels of school and that education was a primary concern within Latino communities. Last, a number of powerful Latino interest groups had begun to demand specific instructional programs, such as bilingual education, English as a second language (ESL), and the teaching of Hispanic culture. At the high school level, Chicano and Mexican students engaged in sit-ins and other forms of civil disobedience to bring attention to racist policies and their educational needs (San Miguel, 2001).

The Bilingual Education Act

Given these contexts, when Texas Senator Ralph Yarborough proposed a four-and-a-half-page bill, known as the Bilingual Education Act (BEA), for consideration as the Title VII amendment to the Elementary and Secondary Education Act of 1965, the social and political climate of the nation was ripe for its passage. Senator Yarborough's original bill was intended to provide assistance to local education agencies for setting up bilingual programs for low-income, native Spanish-speaking children for whom English was a foreign language. By midyear, however, there was considerable pressure placed on the senator to expand the assistance to all low-income, non-English-speaking groups in the United States, which he did in order to pass the bill through the Senate. President Lyndon Johnson signed the bill into law on January 2, 1968, making bilingual education a federal policy for the first time in the history of the United States.

The BEA defined bilingual education as a federal policy "to provide financial assistance to local educational agencies to carry out new and imaginative elementary and secondary school programs" to meet the special educational needs of "children who are educationally disadvantaged because of their inability to speak English" (PL 90-247, Sec. 702). Although the BEA of 1968 did not specifically mandate or define the kinds of programs that schools should use, grants were awarded only to applicants who (1) developed and operated bilingual programs for low-income, non-English-speaking students, (2) made efforts to attract and retain bilingual teachers, and (3) established communication between the home and the school.

AMENDMENTS TO BEA POLICY

Several important changes to the original BEA policy occurred in the 1970s. The first major change was initiated in 1970, when the Office of Civil Rights sent a formal memorandum to school districts serving limited English proficient students (Malakoff & Hakuta, 1990). The memorandum spelled out the conditions of Title VI of the Civil Rights Act of 1964 in relation to students of English as a second language, noting that a Title VI review team had found "a number of practices which have the effect of denying equality of educational opportunity to Spanish-surnamed pupils" and that these practices "have the effect of discrimination on the basis of national origin" (35 *Federal Register,* 11595, 1970). The memorandum also specified that school districts must take affirmative steps to rectify language deficiencies in cases where "the inability to speak and understand English excludes national origin minority group children from effective participation in the educational program" (35 *Federal Register,* 11595, 1970). The memorandum did not specify what the "affirmative steps" should be nor did it make any mention whatsoever of teaching students in their native language (Malakoff & Hakuta, 1990).

The Beginning of Legal Battles

The Office of Civil Rights memorandum set the stage for a series of major legal battles over the legal obligation of school districts receiving federal funds to comply with Title VI guidelines. The single most important legal decision came from the case known as *Lau v. Nichols.* In 1970, a class-action suit filed by the parents of Kenny Lau, a non-English-speaking Chinese child who was forced to attend an English-speaking school as a result of the ruling from *Brown v. Board of*

Education. Kenny had been attending an all-Chinese-speaking school, which was eliminated because all instruction was in Chinese. Kenny Lau and other Chinese families attending San Francisco public school filed a class-action suit in which they claimed that Chinese children were being denied equal educational opportunity because they could not understand or participate when the language of school was solely in English. The school district had identified 2,856 non-English-speaking children, but provided ESL instruction to fewer than half of them. The school district did not dispute the number of students in need of special attention, nor that it had attempted to serve the needs of this population. The issue of the suit was whether non-English-speaking children were able to receive an equal education in an English-only mainstream classroom and whether the school district had a legal obligation to provide special instructional programs to meet the needs of these children. The federal district court ruled in favor of the school district, finding that, because the non-English-speaking children were receiving the *same curriculum in the same class-rooms as English-speaking children*, they were being treated no differently and thus were not being discriminated against by the school district. Accordingly, the court ruled that the school district was under no obligation to provide special services to Kenny Lau and other non-English-speaking students. Instead, the court encouraged the school district to address the program as an educational rather than a legal obligation to the students (August & García, 1988). The ruling was appealed to the Ninth Circuit District Court of Appeals, which upheld the lower court's decision on January 8, 1973. But the dispute did not end there. The case was appealed to and eventually decided upon by the Supreme Court in the following year.

In 1972, a federal district court in New Mexico had addressed the same legal issues in a case involving Mexican American children in the Portales Municipal School district. In *Serna v. Portales Municipal Schools*, however, the court found that non-English-speaking Mexican American children were being treated *differently* when they received the same curriculum as native English-speaking children and thus were being discriminated against (Malakoff & Hakuta, 1990). In response to the ruling, the school district submitted a nonbilingual plan as a remedy to the problem, but the court rejected it, based on expert testimony presented at the court hearing. The school district appealed to the Tenth Circuit Court of Appeals, which in 1974 ruled in favor of the plaintiffs, finding that the students' Title VI rights had been violated and that as a result they had a right to bilingual education.

The Supreme Court handed down the *Lau v. Nichols* decision in favor of the non-English-speaking students and their parents in 1974. The Supreme Court justices avoided the constitutional question of equal protection (the 14th Amendment), and instead, as in *Serna v. Portales Municipal Schools,* relied heavily on Title VI of the Civil Rights Act of 1964 and the Office of Civil Rights memorandum issued in 1970. The court found that guidelines outlined in the 1970 Office of Civil Rights memorandum "clearly indicate that affirmative efforts to give special training for non-English-speaking pupils are required by Title VI as a condition to federal aid to public schools" (414 U.S. 569). Moreover, the court found that students with limited knowledge of English who are submersed in mainstream classes are "effectively foreclosed from any meaningful education" (414 U.S. 566).

The *Lau* decision did not impose any particular educational remedy, such as (native language) bilingual education or English-as-a-second-language instruction. Instead, the court recommended that school districts take into account the numbers of students involved when making decisions concerning an appropriate remedy, suggesting that a remedy may differ from setting to setting.

For those school districts wishing to establish or continue with federally funded bilingual education programs, there were new guidelines to follow under the 1974 amendment to the BEA, which in effect provided the first governmental definition of bilingual education, choosing to define it in transitional terms as "instruction given in, and study of English, and to the extent necessary to allow a child to progress effectively through the education system, the Native language" (Schneider, 1976, pp. 436–437).

The Equal Educational Opportunity Act

In the same year, following the *Lau* decision, Congress legislated the Supreme Court ruling into the Equal Educational Opportunity Act (EEOA) of 1974. The major effect of this new legislation was to extend the *Lau* decision to all public school districts, not just those receiving federal funds. As of 1974, a school district with students who are speakers of languages other than English in any one of its schools is required to "take appropriate action to overcome language barriers that impede equal participation by its students in its instructional programs" (20 U.S.C. Sec. 1703(f)). Section 1703(f) of the EEOA was especially significant because it addressed the issue of "discriminatory effect" vs.

"discriminatory intent" (Malakoff & Hakuta, 1990), declaring that schools could be in violation of Title VI of the Civil Rights Act if English language learners were not receiving some sort of special instructional remedy (discriminatory effect) *even if no substantial intent to discriminate was found.* Following the pattern of earlier legislation, however, the EEOA did not single out any particular instructional remedy as appropriate, leaving the choice between transitional bilingual education and English-as-a-second-language programs up to the local districts. Moreover, in the ensuing years, the power of Section 1703(f) has become increasingly diluted as the courts have continually ruled that local districts would not be subject to taking "appropriate action" without first having the opportunity for due process; that is, to be heard on a case-by-case basis (McFadden, 1983).

The Lau Remedies

Also in 1974, in the wake of the *Lau* decision, the Department of Health, Education and Welfare appointed a task force to establish guidelines for implementing the decision. The guidelines, issued in 1975 under the name *Lau Remedies,* directed school districts having 20 or more students of the same language group having a primary language other than English (1) to establish a means for identifying all students whose primary language is not English, (2) to evaluate the English-language proficiency of these students, and (3) to provide them with appropriate bilingual education programs.

However, since the guidelines were applied only to districts found to be out of compliance with Title VI or the EEOA, their application has been sporadic (Malakoff & Hakuta, 1990). Moreover, Avila and Godoy (1979) point out that when cases are brought to trial, the courts are inclined to examine the guidelines in terms of the ratio between the number of English learners and the total school population. Thus, a large school system may not be required to implement a bilingual program for its students who are speakers of languages other than English even though the number of these students exceeds the minimum specified in the Lau Remedies. Nonetheless, the Remedies remain in effect today, albeit in a threadlike capacity, and together with Section 1703(f) of the EEOA of 1974, they continue as the primary legal force in supporting the rights of English learners to have access to special language programs under certain

■ **Reflection**
Think about your high school experience. If there were English learners in your school, and the school did not provide English support services, do you think this would be a violation of those students' civil rights? Why or why not?

circumstances. Under recent federal policy (e.g., Goals 2000 and No Child Left Behind), coupled with a more conservative federal judicial bench, reference to and the applicability of these legal foundations has been absent.

OTHER CHANGES IN HIGH SCHOOLS

Among other the differences between early and present-day high schools is the new government-directed standardization of curriculum and the increasing use of high-stakes exit exams for high school graduation. To combat criticisms by anti-bilingual conservatives that federally funded programs such as Title VII (bilingual education) and Title I (funding for schools serving high numbers of poor children) promoted fragmentation (recall the unifying function above) and low expectations for achievement, President Clinton issued the Goals 2000: Educate America Act in 1994. This act shifted funding priorities within Title I and Title VII from specific programs to schoolwide improvement plans for augmenting the education of all children and, in particular, for ensuring that the needs and strengths of English learners were being addressed as part of the vision (Coady, Hamann, Harrington, Pacheco, Pho, & Yedlin, 2003). Goals 2000 provided the direction and financial support for a national standards movement, which required states to define in rather specific language what students should know and be able to do at grades 4, 8, and 12.

No Child Left Behind

In 2001, President George W. Bush implemented the No Child Left Behind (NCLB) policy, which dismantled Title VII, and replaced it with Title III, the English Language Acquisition, Language Enhancement, and Academic Achievement Act. Title III relies on formula grants provided to State Education agencies who then distribute funding to school districts on the basis of their English learner student populations (Ovando et al., 2003). For the first time in the history of U.S. public schools, NCLB tied federal money earmarked for education to a nationwide specification of grade level standards for English language arts and mathematics (now used in 49 of 50 states) and increased levels of uniform accountability for teacher effectiveness and for what children and adolescents from diverse language, socioeconomic, and ethnic backgrounds should learn in English in both wealthy and poor urban, suburban, and rural schools (Coady et al., 2003).

New Standards for Graduation

For high schools, NCLB means that secondary teachers across the nation are now required to teach specific English language arts and mathematics content standards and are held strictly accountable for ensuring that their students, regardless of their English-language proficiency, pass a high school exit exam based on those standards in order to graduate. By 2005, 20 states had this requirement in place, with another 5 phasing in exit exams by 2009 (Center on Education Policy, 2004). Among these 25 states requiring an exit exam are Arizona, California, New Mexico, New York, and Texas, states with large and growing populations of immigrant English learners (Waggoner, 1999; Suárez-Orozco, 2005). Significantly, these are also states with high numbers of immigrant students who leave or drop out of school (Orfield, 2004).

HOW SOME HIGH SCHOOLS ARE DEALING WITH ENGLISH LEARNERS: A RESEARCH VIEW

Research on promising practices and good programs for English learners over the past 30 years has concentrated for the most part on what works well with younger children learning English in elementary school communities (see Faltis & Wolfe, 1999; Faltis, 2006). This early focus on elementary school makes sense because that is where most English learners were concentrated and perceived to be in greatest need of support, both pedagogically and legally. Beginning in 1990, however, a small number of researchers in bilingual education turned their attention toward the experiences of English language learners in the secondary schools (middle and high school) for two main reasons: First, because most English learners nationwide were not served by any type of bilingual or English-as-a-second-language program, many students continued to need English-language and literacy support once they entered secondary school (Minicucci & Olsen, 1992). Second, the numbers of secondary-age English learners (13–19) increased considerably throughout the 1980s and 1990s (Waggoner, 1999), reaching unprecedented highs, especially among Spanish-speaking groups (Shin, 2005).

Exemplary Language Minority High Schools

The first major effort to understand effective ways to address the needs of English learners at the secondary level by paying attention to school-wide features was published in 1990. Lucas, Henze, and Donato (1990) studied six exemplary high school programs in California and Arizona with an eye toward documenting the kinds of support systems and pedagogical features that were present in varying degrees across all school settings. They found multiple features that promoted the achievement of English learners in high school (see Table 1.1).

This bellwether study illustrates some of the steps that secondary schools can take to improve the academic success of adolescent English learners. A closer look at the features will reveal that what the six high schools did was what good high schools also do nation-wide (Lightfoot, 1983; Ancess, 2004). However, most high schools do not make the commitments that Lucas, Henze, and Donato (1990) found.

High Schools that Underserve Language Minority Students

In California, the state with the largest number of immigrant English learners, Minicucci and Olsen (1992) studied 23 high schools and found that a majority of them severely underserved English learners (see Table 1.2). They found that the high schools with large numbers of immigrant English learners placed these students at risk of leaving school before graduation because there were few support systems and teachers were not prepared to teach English learners.

As a result of this study, Minicucci and Olsen made four recommendations, which are just as applicable today as they were in 1992: (1) establishment of state-supported, locally based networks to share information about what works in secondary school for English learners; (2) comprehensive staff development focused on the improvement of instruction for English learners; (3) increase in state funding for improving programs and instruction for English learners; and (4) initiative by the State Department of Education to bring practitioners together to promote effective programs and instruction at the secondary level. This book addresses the first two recommendations by focusing on improving instruction for immigrant English learners at the secondary level.

■ **Reflection**
Review the two tables. Which features are evident (or not) in the high school in which you are presently interning or teaching? What measures could be taken to improve your present school site for meeting the needs of English learners?

Table 1.1

Features of High Schools that Promote the Achievement of Immigrant English Learners

IMMIGRANT STUDENTS' LANGUAGES AND CULTURES ARE VALUED AND THE EDUCATION OF ENGLISH LEARNERS IS A TOP PRIORITY

- Teachers learn about students' prior language and schooling experiences
- The school hires bilingual staff with similar cultural experiences of students
- Immigrant students are encouraged to develop and maintain their native language and literacy abilities
- Teachers are knowledgeable about teaching English learners
- The school offers advanced and honors classes taught especially for English learners
- The school makes it possible for English learners to exit English-as-a-second-language programs with strong academic literacy
- The school pays attention to peer social cultural capital to foster positive intergroup relations and interaction across ethnic and social class groupings
- Teachers are expected to provide challenging activities for English learners

THE SCHOOL OFFERS A VARIETY OF PROGRAMS AND COURSES FOR ENGLISH LEARNERS

- A wide range of bilingual, English-as-a-second-language, and sheltered content classes are offered
- Transitional English-as-a-second-language courses support students as they transition into all-English classes
- Immigrant English learners are taught ways to navigate college preparatory curriculum in preparation for postsecondary education

COUNSELORS AND COMMUNITY LIAISONS GIVE SPECIAL ATTENTION TO ENGLISH LEARNERS

- Counselors speak students' languages and share their cultural backgrounds
- Counselors inform English learners of postsecondary educational opportunities
- Counselors believe, emphasize, and monitor academic success of English learners
- Counselors support interaction across ethnic and social class groupings

PARENTS AND COMMUNITY OF ENGLISH LEARNERS ARE INFORMED OF AND INVOLVED IN SCHOOL GOALS AND ACTIVITIES

- School provides and encourages on-campus English-as-a-second-language classes for parents
- School maintains monthly parents' meeting at various times of the day and evening
- School makes sure parents understand grading and standardized assessment policies and procedures
- School encourages parents to work with counselors for planning course schedules
- School actively seeks to disrupt social inequality in course offerings

(Developed from Lucas, Henze, and Ponato, 1990; Ancess, 2004.)

These early research efforts spawned an increased interest in secondary schools, resulting in numerous studies throughout the 1990s. We will only highlight a few of them in this chapter, as our purpose is to show that there is a solid research base for the commitments in practice we highlight in this book.

Table 1.2

Features of High Schools that Place Immigrant English Learners at Risk of Leaving Before Graduation and In Which Immigrant English Learners Do Poorly Academically

TEACHERS WHO WITH LITTLE OR NO BACKGROUND IN TEACHING ACADEMIC CONTENT TO ENGLISH LEARNERS ARE ASSIGNED TO CLASSES WITH LARGE NUMBERS OF ENGLISH LEARNERS

- Teachers with proficiency in a non-English language (but with no English-as-a-second-language experience) are assigned to teach English learners
- English-as-a-second-language teachers without content area expertise are assigned to teach English learners
- New teachers without preparation in English as a second language often teach English learners

ENGLISH LEARNERS ARE OFFERED SPARSE COVERAGE OF ACADEMIC COURSES

- There are large gaps in academic content area courses, especially those needed for graduation
- English learners spend most of their time in English-as-a-second language classes and elective courses
- Core courses are not offered in English learners' primary language or as sheltered content courses
- Immigrant students and English learners are placed and kept in lower academic tracks throughout their secondary school experience

ENGLISH LEARNERS WITH CONVERSATIONAL PROFICIENCY IN ENGLISH ARE LINGUISTICALLY AND SOCIALLY ISOLATED FROM ENGLISH SPEAKERS

- Teachers limit participation of English learners placed in mainstream classes
- No plan exists for integrating English learners with English speakers

PROGRAMS FOR ENGLISH LEARNERS ARE NOT CONSIDERED PART OF SCHOOL COMMUNITY

- No single person is in charge of a comprehensive plan for English learner programs
- English learner programs are little more than a set of English-as-a-second-language courses
- Little communication or coordination exists between department chairs and English-as-a-second-language faculty
- English learners' needs are not considered in the master scheduling plans

LITTLE OR NO SITE LEADERSHIP IS PROVIDED FOR THE NEEDS OF ENGLISH LEARNERS

- The site administrator is not actively responsible for English learners programs and staff
- The responsibility for English learner needs is not shared equally among staff and administration
- There is no sense of a schoolwide response to the needs of English learners

ADDITIONAL SUPPORT MECHANISMS FOR ENGLISH LEARNERS AND THEIR PARENTS ARE NOT PROVIDED

- Academic counselors who speak English learners' primary languages or share their cultural backgrounds are not available
- Bilingual teachers are sparse
- Interaction across ethnic and social class groupings are ignored
- English learners' families and communities are not involved in school activities and are largely uninformed about grading and standardized assessment policies and procedures

(Developed from Minicucci & Olsen, 1992; Minicucci, 1995; Oakes & Rogers, 2006.)

RECENT RESEARCH ON SECONDARY PROGRAMS FOR ENGLISH LEARNERS

In 1993, several publications included research on secondary bilingual programs and practices. The first major publication to include a chapter on secondary bilingual education was published by the National Society for the Study of Education (Arias & Casanova, 1993). This was a collection of essays on bilingual education. That same year a theme issue of the *Peabody Journal of Education*, edited by Faltis (1993), was dedicated to articles about secondary bilingual programs. Late in 1993, the *Proceedings of the Third National Research Symposium on Limited English Proficient Student Issues: Focus on Middle and High School Issues* was published. This added a significant number of studies to the field.

The California Tomorrow Report

Between 1993 and the turn of the century, a number of studies were published pertaining to English learners at the secondary level. In 1994, Olsen published a *California Tomorrow Research and Policy Report*, which focused on an extensive study of 32 randomly selected secondary schools. The study was shaped by three issues: (1) changing demographics require changes in schools; (2) research has documented inequalities rooted in institutional structures; and (3) new challenges require new thinking about secondary schools and support for educators engaged in the change process. The following year, Minicucci (1995) published a report on eight case studies of exemplary secondary schools. In these schools, Minicucci found that English learners were able to learn the same academic curriculum as native English speakers as long as there were support systems in place. Common school characteristics included a schoolwide vision of excellence, creation of a community of learners engaged in active discovery, and well-designed, carefully executed language-development programs.

An Ethnographic Study

In 1996, Olsen conducted an ethnographic study of an urban high school in California examining the ways in which English language learners adapt to an increasingly multicultural school environment. She uncovered that the school was divided into three unconnected groups: recent immigrants, all other students, and the faculty and administration. This division contributed to the marginalization of English language learners. She found that English learners were tracked into low-level classes, separated from English speakers, provided with inadequate instruction and instructional materials, and denied access to core content areas.

Olsen followed up her study with publication of *Made in America* (1997), which poignantly narrates versions of the lived experiences of immigrant students, their teachers, and classmates within the context of an urban high school in California. Olsen found that although each version contested the other two, the separate versions worked together to produce a "racializing process of Americanization" (Olsen, 1997, p. 240). For Olsen, the racializing process of Americanization for immigrant students both created and resulted in (1) the exclusion and separation of immigrant students academically, placing these students in classes with little access to English-speaking peers or in classes with poorly prepared teachers; (2) pressure on immigrant students to relinquish their national identity and first language while simultaneously being pressured to become Americanized; and (3) taking a place in the school's racialized structures, which affiliated immigrant students with others who were like them, which consequently contributed to a continuation of racial tracking and inadequate schooling for them.

A Collection of Studies

Faltis and Wolfe (1999) produced an edited volume of research-based studies on immigrant adolescents in secondary school, covering topics ranging from adolescent immigrant gender issues and teaching writing to immigrant students to programmatic structural concern and the preparation of secondary teachers of immigrant students. This volume pointed to a number of issues that continue to be of concern for high schools and teachers of immigrant adolescents, and offered answers that are contextualized within the studies they represented.

School Connections

Many immigrant and English learners fail to align themselves with peers who are connected to the mainstream of school life. In an edited volume of studies about Mexican immigrants and children of Mexican immigrants, Gibson, Gándara, and Koyama (2004) look into the roles of peer relations, peer pressure, and peer influence on becoming and staying connected in secondary school. Gibson and her colleagues describe and attempt to explain peer influence and the ways in which teachers and other school personnel mediate how peers both help and hinder school achievement among Mexican-origin youth. Their research suggests that "when appropriate and welcoming spaces are not created for marginalized students, they will create alternative spaces for belonging," even when these alternative spaces lead to identities that are in opposition to those valued for academic success (Gibson et al., 2004, p. 12).

The Futures Project

At Wilson High School in Los Angeles, immigrant students, English learners, and minority students (Chicanos and African Americans) were routinely placed into lower tracks, channeling students toward futures that were quite different from those of students placed in honor tracks. Oakes and Rogers (2006) describe how the principal and faculty of Wilson high experimented with more inclusive strategies to help immigrant and minority students prepare for and navigate a more demanding college preparatory curriculum. The Futures Project at Wilson High School was not able to successfully disrupt the inherently inequitable tracking system that existed in the school. Nonetheless, Oakes and Rogers learned that considerable steps could be taken to improve education for immigrants, minorities, and English learners when the principal and faculty make a concerted effort to address social inequities in school programs. The Futures Project points to various ways secondary schools with large immigrant English learner and minority students can learn to contend with challenges and obstacles, develop networks of support and information, gain critical understanding of educational inequality, and focus on career aspirations that are often denied them.

COMMON THREADS IN RESEARCH

The research in secondary education for English learners is still relatively scant. As a result of a recent surge in studies in the last 10 years, however, there are some well-defined implications and some common threads that we can surely learn from (Coulter, 2003). How well do you think high schools are doing with respect to meeting the needs of adolescent immigrant English learners? What can we learn from the research on secondary English learners programs and practices? What steps can we take to disrupt inequality in schools? In this final section, we lay out what we see as common threads throughout the research we highlighted. In most high schools, the following patterns occurred:

1. *Access.* English language learners are not given equal access to the dominant ways of doing, saying, and believing in core curriculum classes, electives, or extracurricular activities in ways that simultaneously value their language and culture.

2. *Tracking.* Immigrant students and English learners are tracked into remedial classes that have low expectations for achievement and that undermine their academic success.

3. *Segregation.* Immigrant students and English learners are physically and socially segregated from their native English-speaking peers throughout the school day and school year.

4. *Ineffective instructional practices.* Instruction used with English learners does not enable them to exchange ideas about academic and social content with each other or their classroom peers. Native language academic content classes are rare. Teachers of English learners are not prepared for effective instruction, even in sheltered content classes in which content and language can be made more accessible to English learners.

5. *Lack of resources.* English learners do not have equal access to resources for classrooms, materials, field trips, and other learning needs.

6. *Compartmentalization.* Secondary schools are compartmentalized in a manner that contributes to the marginalization of English language learners.

7. *Assimilation.* English learners are expected to assimilate to the dominant culture, leaving behind their own language and cultural identities.

8. *Cultural irrelevance.* There is little cultural relevance for many English learners in either the instruction or the institution of school.

> **■ Reflection**
>
> What do you consider the best arguments for providing appropriate educational support for immigrant English learners? Why might parents of high achieving English-speaking students resist efforts to improve schooling for English learners by placing them in college preparatory classes instead of lower tracks?

In the next chapter, we spell out the commitments in practice that we believe address these patterns of failure on the part of secondary schools to meet the needs of adolescent immigrant English learners. Chapter 2 is especially important because it provides you with a way to understand and act on commitments in practice that work to the benefit of English learners, and thus to the benefit of all students in secondary school.

Summary

One of the main purposes of secondary school in America has been to create a unified educated class built on a common set of knowledge and understandings about American (and European) history, literature, math, and science. Early on, secondary schools overtly functioned to Americanize newcomers, but there has always been serious debate about the extent to which secondary school should make adjustments for the language and culture of students who enter school with little or no proficiency in English. Although there was no hesitation to exclude African American, Mexicans, and Native Americas up until the mid-20th century, secondary schools continue to wrestle with what to do with new immigrants and English learners. In this chapter, we reviewed some of the historical, legal, and educational foundations of secondary education in the United States. Key points to draw out of this chapter are as follows:

- The *Cardinal Principles of Secondary Education* spelled out the role of secondary schools as agents of Americanization for newcomer immigrant students.
- Americanization efforts are particularly high when immigrants are perceived to be different from the mainstream.
- Americanization efforts intensify during and after major wars.
- In the late 1960s and 1970s, legal and political climates facilitated the introduction of bilingual education as an educational remedy for immigrant students and English learners.
- Much of what is known about bilingual and English-as-a-second-language education comes from studies in elementary education conducted in the 1970s and 1980s.
- Research in secondary education on effective programs and practices began in the early 1990s.
- The No Child Left Behind Act of 2001 tied federal money to standards-based curricula and implemented high-stakes testing for high school graduation, a move that has had serious consequences for secondary immigrant students and English learners.
- Recent research in secondary schools with large immigrant and English learner populations reveals some of the factors that help and hinder the academic success of immigrant students and English learners.

Knowing about the historical, political, and educational reasons for teaching immigrant students and English learners in their native language and through English is an important part of being an educated teacher and an advocate for English learners.

References

Ancess, J. (2004). *Beating the odds: High schools as communities of commitment.* New York: Teachers College Press.

Arias, B., & Casanova, U. (Eds.). (1993). *Bilingual education: Politics, practice, research.* Chicago: National Society for the Study of Education.

August, D., & García, E. (1988). *Language minority education in the United States.* Springfield, IL: Charles C. Thomas.

Avila, J. G., & Godoy, R. (1979). Bilingual/bicultural education and the law. In National Dissemination and Assessment Center (Ed.), *Language development in a bilingual setting* (pp. 15–33). Los Angeles: California State University.

Center on Education Policy. (2004). *State high school exams: A maturing reform.* Washington, DC: Author.

Coady, M., Hamann, E., Harrington, M., Pacheco, M., Pho, S. & Yedlin, J. (2003). *Claiming opportunities: A handbook for improving education for English language learners through comprehensive school reform.* Providence, RI: The Education Alliance at Brown University.

Coulter, C. (2003). *Snow White, revolutions, the American dream and other fairy tales: Growing up immigrant in an American high school.* Unpublished doctoral dissertation, Arizona State University, Tempe, Arizona.

Cuban, L. (1993). *How teachers taught: Constancy and change in American classrooms, 1890–1990.* New York: Teachers College Press.

Faltis, C. (Ed.). (1993). Trends in bilingual education at the secondary level. *Peabody Journal of Education, 69*(1).

Faltis, C. (2006). *Teaching English language learners in elementary school communities: A join-fostering approach.* Columbus, OH: Merrill/Pearson Education.

Faltis, C., & Wolfe, P. (Eds.). (1999). *So much to say: Adolescents, bilingualism & ESL in the secondary school.* New York: Teachers College Press.

Flores, S., & Murillo, E. (2001). Power, language, and ideology: Historical and contemporary notes on the dismantling of bilingual education. *The Urban Review, 33*(3), 183–206.

Gibson, M., Gándara, P., & Koyama, J. P. (Eds.). (2004). *School connections: U.S. Mexican youth, peers, and school achievement.* New York: Teachers College Press.

Jacobs, J. F., & Pierce, M. L. (1966). Bilingualism and creativity. *Elementary English, 43,* 1390–1400.

Judd, E. L. (1978). *Factors affecting the passage of the Bilingual Education Act of 1967.* Doctoral dissertation, New York University.

Lambert, W. E., & Peal, E. (1962). The relationship of bilingualism to intelligence. *Psychological Monographs, 76,* 1–23.

Lightfoot, S. L. (1983). *The good high school: Portraits of character and culture.* New York: Basic Books.

Lucas, T., Henze, R., & Donato, R. (1990). Promoting the success of Latino language minority students: An exploratory study of six high schools. *Harvard Educational Review, 60*(3), 315–340.

Malakoff, M., & Hakuta, K. (1990). History of language minority education in the United States. In A. M. Padilla, H. H. Fairchild, & C. M. Valadez (Eds.), *Bilingual education: Issues and strategies* (pp. 27–44). Newbury Park, CA: Sage.

McFadden, B. J. (1983). Bilingual education and the law. *Journal of Law and Education, 12*(1), 1–27.

Minicucci, C. (1995). School reform and student diversity. *Phi Delta Kappan, 71*(1), 77–80.

Minicucci, C., & Olsen, L. (1992). *Programs for secondary limited English proficient students: A California study.* Washington, DC: National Clearinghouse for Bilingual Education.

Oakes, J., & Rogers, J. (2006). *Learning power: Organizing for education and justice.* New York: Teachers College Press.

Olsen, L. (1994). *California Tomorrow Research and Policy Report.* San Francisco: California Tomorrow.

Olsen, L. (1996). *The unfinished journey: Restructuring schools in a diverse society.* San Francisco: California Tomorrow.

Olsen, L. (1997). *Made in America: Immigrant students in our public schools.* New York: The New Press.

Orfield, G. (Ed.). (2004). *Dropouts in America: Confronting the graduation rate crisis.* Cambridge, MA: Harvard Education Press.

Ovando, C., Collier, V., & Combs, M. C. (2003). *Bilingual & ESL classrooms: Teaching in multicultural contexts.* Boston: McGraw Hill.

San Miguel, Jr., Guadalupe (2001). *Brown, not white: School integration and the Chicano movement in Houston.* College Station, TX: Texas A&M University Press.

Schneider, S. G. (1976). *Revolution, reaction or reform: The 1974 bilingual education act.* New York: Las Americas.

Shin, H. (2005, May). *School enrollment—Social and economic characteristics of students: October, 2003.* Washington, DC: U.S. Census Bureau, Current Population Reports.

Suárez-Orozco, M. (2005, February). *Moving stories: Rethinking immigration and education in the global era.* Paper presented at the International Conference on Sociology of Education, Silomar, California.

Tyack, D. (1974). *The one best system: A history of American urban education.* Cambridge, MA: Harvard University Press.

Waggoner, D. (1999). Who are secondary newcomer and linguistically different youth? In C. Faltis & P. Wolfe (Eds.), *So much to say: Adolescents, bilingualism and ESL in the secondary school* (pp. 13–41). New York: Teachers College Press.

Wraga, W. (1994). *Democracy's high school: The comprehensive high school and educational reform in the United States.* Lanham, MD: University Press of America.

2 Commitments in Practice

Scott Cunningham/Merrill

OVERVIEW

This chapter presents the theoretical principles of teaching and learning for you to use when planning, implementing, and evaluating your academic content lessons and classroom activities. The guiding questions for this chapter are:

- How can theory help you with teaching in ways that ensure immigrant students and English learners participate fully in your classes?
- What are some of the key sociocultural dynamics of classroom life involved in language and content learning?
- What are communities of practice and how do they relate to language and content learning?
- What is the role of identity creation and affiliation in language and content learning?
- What are commitments in practice that can help you plan and organize your classroom discussions and activities so that students learn language during content instruction?

The theoretical principles we present are especially applicable to inviting and engaging English learners, but they are relevant for all students. Theory provides us with explanations and understandings to guide our thinking, our actions, and our beliefs about why something happens or is likely to happen. Theory is behind everything that happens inside a classroom. It is based on what people believe they understand about how something works. Every time you or your students think about and discuss ideas, there are theoretical principles that organize how thinking, behaving, and discussing unfold. For example, when students calculate a standard deviation, examine a historical document for time-period evidence, or discuss the author's motives for portraying a character as capricious, theory is involved.

In high school, each academic content area is organized generally to provide major ideas, theorems, procedures, questions, and supporting information, and more specifically to engage learners in ways of thinking, talking, acting, and believing that are considered to be appropriate for that academic content. In later chapters, we will discuss in more detail the academic dimensions of talk, interaction, and participation within four academic content areas: social studies, language arts, mathematics, and science. If you are a physical education teacher, an art teacher, a music teacher, or drama teacher, do not despair or feel disregarded. The theoretical principles, what we refer to as "commitments," presented in this chapter are the foundations for how to invite adolescent English learners to participate fully in your classrooms, regardless of the academic content or set of social and academic practices associated with that content. We focus on the above four academic content areas because these are the ones that are most related to successful graduation and preparation for college. To repeat, our purpose is to help you become more knowledgeable and able to invite adolescent immigrant English learners into classroom activities, so that they can participate as welcomed members of the classroom. In this chapter we present and elaborate on five commitments in practice that we will highlight in subsequent chapters to show how you can use them to guide your teaching, learning, and assessment. We begin with a brief discussion on our theoretical stance and then proceed to what "commitments in practice" means.

OUR THEORETICAL STANCE ON LEARNING ENGLISH IN SECONDARY SCHOOL

One of the distinguishing features of this book is the particular theoretical perspective we take on how immigrant students and English learners acquire English in secondary school and become successful academically. Our perspectives do not rely on models of second language acquisition that are used extensively in elementary education settings. We know from experiences at the secondary level and years of study and research that learning a second language and learning through a second language is largely a sociocultural challenge, involving student investments, identity alignments, and participation in academic communities of practice.

Some of you might be familiar with Stephen Krashen's Monitor Theory and Jim Cummins's distinction between basic interpersonal communication skills (BICS) and cognitive academic language proficiency (CALP), as these theoretical perspectives permeate many of the approaches to teaching English learners at the elementary level. These perspectives are grounded in cognitive psychology, where the individual learner and what happens inside his or her head is central. Krashen (1982) argues that teachers should be concerned with *acquisition* (unconscious learning, where the focus is on meaning), not *learning* (conscious learning, where the focus is on form). For him, students acquire a second language by receiving *comprehensible input*, language adjusted slightly beyond the learner's current level of proficiency. Krashen also acknowledges the importance of providing learners with a safe and comfortable acquisition environment. In such an environment, the learners will have an open affective filter, which enables comprehensible input to be processed in the learner's language acquisition device, something that all humans possess. Learners continue to acquire their new language to the extent they receive continued doses of comprehensible input. One of the ways they get new comprehensible input is by using their newly acquired language to communicate, which necessarily solicits more comprehensible input.

Cummins (1979) argues that learners who acquire basic conversational language are not necessarily equipped to succeed in academic settings, where language, according to him, requires more cognitive operations than are involved in interpersonal communication. For Cummins, school language requires a cognitively developed kind of language ability that goes beyond any abilities that can be acquired through comprehensible input alone. Cummins argues that CALP involves using language in ways that require students to analyze, synthesize, summarize, and otherwise manipulate language in ways that are not typically done when students interact about personal topics.

We reject both of these theoretical perspectives as being overly linked to cognitive psychology, where the concern is limited to what goes on in the head of the learner to the exclusion of social contexts in which learners live and participate. We approach learning, as you will see below, from sociocultural perspectives. From our vantage point, Krashen's ideas fail to address the complex and often socially unjust lives of English learners inside classrooms, where context, identity affiliations, peer relations, and interaction around academic content are socially and culturally constructed. We believe that teaching immigrant students and English learners requires commitments in practices focused on enhancing participation in ways that break down social barriers and help students learn language while they are learning content. This is not to say that making language understandable and engaging learners in challenging activities are not worthwhile goals. For us, making language understandable means that English learners understand how to use language in the multiple ways that are recognized as appropriate for the academic content they are learning, including both conversational and academic ways of using language. Making this happen requires a deeper understanding of the sociocultural dynamics of language and content learning in classroom settings. For extensive discussion of issues involving cognitive approaches to second language acquisition (SLA), we recommend Block (2003), Hawkins (2004), and Watson-Gegeo (2004); for extensive reviews of Cummins, see Edelsky (2006) and MacSwan (2000).

COMMITMENTS IN PRACTICE

We refer to theoretical principles for inviting immigrant students and English learners into your classroom communities as *commitments in practice*. Commitments are stances in the form of pledges that we make regarding how to approach and treat people and other living organisms, events, beliefs, and actions. A commitment is stronger than a personal belief or opinion; it is based on a solemn promise to do and act in a certain way for reasons of ethics, justice, morality, and values. With respect to teaching immigrant English learners, commitments have to do with pledging that your behavior and the behavior of English-speaking students in the classroom respect the learning needs of immigrant students (ethics); that you and English-speaking students learn to do the right things for immigrant students in your classroom (morality); that you, other staff members, and English-speaking students treat immigrant students fairly (justice); and that you provide immigrant students with challenging and engaging activities that value their prior knowledge and participation (values). Another way to understand commitments is to ask yourself the following questions:

- Does what I do in class support all learners, including immigrant English learners?
- Are all of the students in my class able to participate equally?
- Do I offer opportunities in my classroom for language and literacy experiences that my students bring to the classroom?
- Do I value, marginalize, or ignore the language and literacy abilities that my students bring to the classroom?
- Do all of the students in my classroom have access to the resources needed to participate in the class activities?
- Does the curriculum I use take into consideration topics and issues about which both immigrant and nonimmigrant students are compelled to investigate?

These questions are a way to think about the kinds of commitments that are needed to make your classrooms more inviting and appropriate for English learners. In this book, we try to show you how some teachers have responded to these questions. We hope that you use these questions in thinking about ways to align your classroom practices with the commitments we present.

Notice that we say *commitments IN practice* as opposed to *commitments TO practice*. We draw attention to this to emphasize that practice always involves theory and theory only exists through practice. The commitments we share have to do with ways of organizing and carrying out teaching and learning as these happen in classrooms and schools. Commitments TO practice are proleptic, anticipatory of what might happen; that is, theory about practice, rather than theory happening in practice. You might think that the difference is nugatory, and that we are quibbling over two very small, insignificant words. Not so, we contend (see Edelsky, 1994, who first discussed the distinction). We want you to commit to improving instruction for English learners *while* you are teaching and *while* they are learning. Accordingly, commitments IN practice show you what happens in classrooms with English learners so that you can not only learn from these experiences, but also identify with them and make them part of your stance toward teaching and learning.

Let us also say a few words about the notion of *practice*. By "practice" in this context, at one level, we mean repeated activities in which students imitate or try out ways of saying, thinking, and doing things in order to acquire proficiency. This is likely how most of you understand the meaning of practice. Of course, English learners need to be engaged in hearing and using English for multiple purposes with different audiences, and they need to practice their English to flourish as learners. At another level, practice means engaging in ways of saying, thinking, and doing that enable learners to try on new identities as members of what are called *communities of practice* (Wenger, 1998).

ACADEMIC COMMUNITIES OF PRACTICE

All students belong to communities of practice in and out of school. Communities of practice are social spaces, knowledge, values, and affinities that people acquire by actively participating in the social practices of particular communities (Wenger, 1998). As people engage in communities of practice they also construct identities in relation to the communities. Communities of practice can be both real and imagined (Kanno & Norton, 2003). In real communities of practice, learners engage in and, in some cases, are apprenticed into the actual practices of the community. For example, if in your teacher education program you were required to intern with a mentor and practice teaching in an actual classroom under his/her guidance over time, you would have been engaged—apprenticed, if you will—into a real community of practice. You also would have been reading about and discussing teaching in your methods classes, and in this way, you would have acquired the understanding and ways of talking about teaching that approached those of your mentor teacher. By participating in this real community of practice, you also would begin to take on an identity of a teacher, using markers of membership that full members recognize and use to show membership in the community of practice. Imagined communities of practice are ways of participating in practices that represent real communities of practice. In imagined communities of practice, learners participate in activities, use language, and gain specific knowledge that reflects what members of real communities of practice do, think, believe, and value. For example, if you did practice teaching in your methods classes in front of your peers, with your professor as the mentor, you participated in an imagined community of practice. In this case, the goal is to enable you to participate in social practices that connect you to real communities of practice and to enable you to further create your identity as a new member in the teaching communities of practice.

The Role of Sociocultural Theory

The idea of practice as creating new identities and becoming new members of real and imagined communities of practice comes from sociocultural theory, which views learning largely as a matter of apprenticeship (Edelsky, Smith, & Wolfe, 2002; Gee, 2004; Lave & Wenger, 1991; Wenger, 1998). From this perspective, new members (English learners) are apprenticed into ways of talking, thinking, believing, acting, and so forth, that are recognized, valued, and used within a community of old timers—teachers and more capable peers (Vygotsky, 1978)—who pass on their knowledge and behaviors to new members.

The ways of talking, thinking, believing, and acting in literature, math, and science classes belong to (are affiliated with) a combination of real communities and imagined communities of practice. For students in your classes, real communities of practice are the tangible ways they study academic content, using language and tools (books, computers, graphic organizers, formulae, photographs, readings, videos, writings, etc.) to gain the knowledge and behaviors into which the teacher as academic community representative invites them. Communities of practice are also the intangible ways that students invest in academic content communities (through discussions, discourse, interactions, and positioning, the extent to which they internalize content into their personal lives, etc.). Part of their participation in academic communities of practice is also imagined. That is, as students are apprenticed into classroom academic communities of practice, they also affiliate with a group of people who are not immediately tangible and accessible; their connections to a community of practice occur through imagination (Kanno & Norton, 2003). In this manner, when students successfully engage in the practices of academic communities, which in turn belong to larger outside communities of practice, they imagine themselves as future members of these outside communities.

Suppose your students were working on a writing assignment, and the English learners in your class were individually coming to you with their quick writes for a one-on-one writing conference. Your goal is twofold: (1) to talk with students about how to write well in English, and (2) to help students "do what writers do" as they edit and revise their writing for clarity, meaning, and audience participation. Both goals are connected to real and imagined communities of practice. Writing well in English means involving and investing students with community practices that provide them membership into large communities; in this case, the community of conventional written English. The second goal aims to involve students in the literary community of practice that has certain rules, patterns, and actions that are authentic within the real community of writers (Wolfe & Faltis, 1999; Wolfe, 2004). In both instances, students create new images of themselves as English learners and writers as they join literary communities of practice. As a result they create a new sense of identity that is twofold: (1) affiliation within real and imagined communities of practice ("I am a scientist, mathematician, artist, historian, etc."); and (2) a sense of themselves as readers ("I read and make sense of what others write") and writers ("I am a writer and I write with and for myself and others").

Communities of Practice in High School

In high school, where there are multiple communities of practice corresponding to content areas that overlap and contribute to one another in complex ways, students enter as newcomers and must be invited into real and imagined communities of practice by engaging in the myriad processes (talking, thinking, writing, drawing, computing, crafting, critiquing, inquiring, feeling, analyzing, reciting, memorizing, role-playing, etc.). This being said, it can be argued that many students in high school are not true newcomers to academic communities of practice, especially if they have gained membership in them in elementary school. Contrariwise, depending on their prior formal schooling experiences and knowledge of English, immigrant English learners are likely to be newcomers to ways of talking about, thinking about, and getting things done *in English* within content areas that rely heavily on cultural knowledge and experience with understanding text. For example, as English learners study new ways of understanding and using arithmetic for measuring plant growth in a science experiment, they are probably engaging in relatively familiar social practices in science and math about which they are already knowledgeable and can imagine themselves doing in other contexts. But, when they read about and discuss the properties of a plant seed and form alternative hypotheses about why plants grow or don't grow without light, this may be a new social practice that requires apprenticeship and affiliation in addition to learning to use oral and written English in specialized new ways. In other words, the discursive properties and social practices in "doing science," such as hypothesizing and problem solving using the scientific method, may be new to English learners (Lemke, 1990). If that is the case, the discourse, behaviors, and interactions around science that are new to English learners are *in addition to* the medium of English. If behaviors such as measuring and adding (which, by the way, are more concrete) are familiar to English learners, these are means through which affiliation to science and math is already present, in spite of the new language.

The Role of Identity in Communities of Practice

One way to grasp the meaning of learning in classroom communities of practice is to think of learning as constantly moving from the peripheral of a community knowledge base to its core or center (Lave & Wenger, 1991). Along the way, newcomers begin to identify themselves as members of the real and imagined community when they appropriate ways of talking about, understanding, and performing in ways that more centrally located members recognize and use for their continuing participation in the community of practice. In this manner, identity and affiliation with others, real and imagined, who also engage in the same kinds of locally situated practice is paramount for continued participation and, ultimately, learning (Kanno & Norton, 2003). By *identity*, we mean how students understand their relationship to the content-area practices in and out of school, how that relationship is created and nurtured across time and space, and how the students understand possibilities for future membership in classroom life, moving from the periphery to the center of communities of practice (Norton, 2000; Hawkins, 2004).

Participation and Nonparticipatory

The concepts of communities of practice and identity construction with real and imagined communities of practice, however, are more complex than moving from the periphery identities to core identities, because as Lave and Wenger (1991) point out, there are "multiple, varied, more or less-engaged and inclusive ways of being located in the fields of participation defined by a community" (p. 36). In other words, learners' relationships to communities of practice necessarily involve participation and nonparticipation, both of which, in combination, create the identities learners create (Wenger, 1998). Nonparticipation is expected in all communities of practice because some of the practices required and imagined in any community will be too far beyond the experiences and abilities learners bring to them.

There is an important difference between nonparticipation and being nonparticipatory in practices within communities to which learners have been invited to belong (Kanno & Norton, 2003). Learners who are nonparticipatory in practices within communities to which they belong see themselves as marginal to the community, and thus, are less likely to gain full membership. It is important to understand that when students are nonparticipatory in academic communities, they are still participatory in other communities of practice— mainly communities that stand in opposition to academic ones.

Learners bring with them to any community of practice existing identities and knowledge that may or may not be recognized by others as important or useful for participation, making access to continued participation in certain communities of practice conflictual for certain learners (Kanno & Applebaum, 1995; Valdés, 2001) and leading to nonparticipatory behaviors. In a classroom setting with multiple sets of relations, identities, and practices, all members are not equal when they are participating in different learning contexts. Some students have struggles for position within certain communities of practice and have more easy access to others. Why might this be the case?

In all classrooms, learners are constantly being positioned and are positioning others through comparisons about how well they participate academically and socially with language and literacy in classroom activities. Predominantly, learners are differentiated through scads of assessments. As teachers, you assess everything from language proficiency to how well students participate in whole group teaching.

You judge how well students speak, understand, read, and write standard English; how well they work independently; how well they work in small groups; how organized their thoughts seem to be as they respond to your questions and queries; how they handle not knowing something; how compliant they are with directives; and how engaged they seem to be at different points in a lesson.

Classmates are also judging the abilities just mentioned, and their judgments also figure into how students are positioned and position themselves as classroom members. In high school, classmates often notice and comment on how well or poorly another student answers the teacher's questions, speaks standard English, writes in English, sits, and follows directions. These assessments contribute to the identities that students assume as they move from one activity to the next.

Learners are also differentiated by physical presentation (Toohey, 2000). Adolescents are identified by classmates and identify with classmates on the basis of clothing style, name brands, hairstyle, skin color, and physical appearance (Matuti-Bianchi, 1986). Students use physical features and abilities to form and re-form friendships both in and out of the classroom. Looking Mexican, Middle Eastern, or "American," wearing certain clothes and clothes brands, and hairstyles all send powerful messages about who learners are and how others perceive them as having certain status and being competent members of the classroom community (Cohen, 1994).

How students in your class interact, behave, and present themselves reveals much about their identities and, consequently, their place in the hierarchies of the classroom community. If academic learning depends on the establishment of certain kinds of social relations that enable participants enough practice in real and imagined community activities to become good at the practices, then it is imperative that you become aware of how students see themselves and how others identify them. In addition, you must also take steps to enable those students who are hindered from academic learning to gain access and feel comfortable participating as who they are. When students are impeded from academic learning, they may join other non-academic-oriented communities of practices in concert with their developing identities (such as gangs or oppositional cliques) or their participation in academic communities of practice may be truncated, feeding into identities associated with low status in the various classroom hierarchies (Cohen, 1994). The commitments in practice that we present below are geared to minimize marginalization and optimize engagement and learning.

COMMITMENTS IN PRACTICE FOR TEACHING ADOLESCENT ENGLISH LEARNERS AND IMMIGRANT STUDENTS

Following are five commitments in practice for inviting immigrant English learners to engage and imagine their participation in academic communities of practice. An abbreviated form is presented in capital letters to refer to particular commitments in practice throughout the book.

1. *English learners must participate actively in classroom activities that involve multiple opportunities for language and literacy use affiliated with academic communities of practice* (ACTIVE PARTICIPATION). By active, we mean that students are engaged socially, emotionally, and intellectually in whatever activity they are doing. Students can be actively listening, selectively attending to key ideas, steps, explanations, and vocabulary. They can be actively figuring out through inference and deduction why something is happening or not as they expected. They can be reading silently, actively making sense of some author's narrative or expository text. They can be writing out notes for later study or making a draft of what they want to explain or devising a chart that shows similarities and differences between two events. They can be questioning or reflecting in journals or learning logs or engaging in discussions about content with classmates. In each of these examples, students are active because they are engaged in practices that use prior knowledge to enter into new language uses and meanings that further their understanding.

   By participation, we mean that students are acting, behaving, thinking, and taking part in goal-oriented, social activities that use language and literacy to further their involvement as members of real and imagined communities of practice. Active participation, therefore, for English learners is being engaged in classroom practices that enable them to act, think, behave, and understand in ways that are aligned with the communities to which the practices belong.

2. *English learners are socially integrated with peers of various language and academic abilities to build on prior knowledge and to scaffold new knowledge* (SOCIAL INTEGRATION). We place a premium on social integration because it has been well documented that immigrant English learners are often segregated from English-speaking peers at the classroom and school level (Kozol, 2005; Minicucci & Olsen,

▲ **Caveat**

This commitment does not apply to recently arrived newcomer immigrants with little or no English proficiency and with little or no experience in formal educational practices. These students should be placed in beginning level English classes and socially integrated with other beginning and early intermediate level English learners at least until they are adjusted to school and attuned to English.

1992; Olsen, 1997; Olsen & Jaramillo, 1999; Ruíz-de-Velasco & Fix, 2000). This commitment in practice stresses the importance in ensuring that immigrant English learners have multiple opportunities to interact using oral and written English among themselves and with English-speaking classmates. Socially integrating immigrant English learners with English-speaking peers can enable students from both groups to draw on, share, and exchange prior knowledge to make sense of new ideas. Because students are talking together, new knowledge will be scaffolded on the spot (supported through clarification, visuals, translations, rephrasing, etc.) when there is misunderstanding or language use that is too far beyond the abilities of one or more of the participants.

Grouping students heterogeneously not only integrates students who might otherwise have minimal contact, but also improves the performance of all members of a learning community. All students have multiple abilities, not just those who speak English, are literate in English, and have prior formal school experience in U.S schools (Cohen, 1994). When students of diverse abilities come together to exchange ideas and help one another, everybody benefits.

In the following chapter, you will learn about Newcomer Centers and Programs for recently arrived immigrants. In later chapters, we discuss methods, strategies, structures, and practices for both whole group and small group settings that socially and physically integrate students with diverse English language and literacy abilities so that they can work together and benefit from their exchanges and practice with English speakers. As you shall see, social integration and using heterogeneous groups requires classroom management planning and structure.

3. *English language learning is integrated throughout academic content activities* (INTEGRATED LANGUAGE LEARNING). This is a cornerstone commitment for you to become language teachers as well as academic content teachers. Because academic activities can be planned to integrate English learners with native English speakers, you can support English language learning by planning for language acquisition to happen as students learn content. In a very real sense, the English used in class acquires English learners as much as English learners acquire English from you and classmates.

In other words, how your classroom is organized to support the acquisition of English language and literacy is a function of your teaching and learning practices. The practices in which you engage students socially construct the kinds of English language and literacy that students acquire. It is in this sense that English acquires learners while learners acquire English. This is not to say, however, that English learners do not have agency; that is, that they don't make investments and choices about how and to what extent they participate and acquire English. We make this point to emphasize that English learners are not like computers, receiving input willy-nilly. Your students who are learning English are people who respond to the invitations to and opportunities for learning that you provide them.

Bearing this in mind, you should plan and organize your classroom discussions and activities so that the language used with students seeks to accomplish three interrelated language goals geared to helping them:

A. Make meaning (make sense of and convey understanding, at times with precision) with oral and written language;

B. Understand how oral and written language operates as codes of language sounds, letters, words, sentence conventions, and cultural meanings to make sense of and convey meaning; and

C. Use oral and written language as tools for learning about academic content in both real and imagined communities of practice (Halliday, 1975).

In later chapters, you will see how the practices occurring in content areas we highlight incorporate these goals. That is, English learners are invited and nudged to make meaning with, learn about, and learn through English while they are actively participating in practices valued and reinforced within the academic and content area communities.

4. *English learners' linguistic and cultural identities and affinities can be strengthened and nurtured in the classroom* (SOCIOCULTURAL IDENTITY SUPPORT). Sociocultural identity formation during adolescence has direct bearing on how well students align themselves with the academic and social learning communities that are populated by students (Gee, 2004; Suárez-Orozco, C., 2005). Immigrant English learners who maintain linguistic and cultural affinities while they become accustomed to U.S. schools and learn

English tend to achieve academically better than immigrant English learners who are forced to relinquish ties to their home countries (Suárez-Orozco, M., 2005; Suárez-Orozco & Todorova, 2003). Sociocultural identity differs from the identities students can create and build on as they engage in academic communities of practice. By sociocultural identity, we mean that students have multiple opportunities to accommodate to new settings, including school, while they maintain who they are without having to assimilate to local sociocultural ways of being in order to be considered successful. As they accommodate without having to assimilate, they add on new ways of doing things and new affinities to their heritage, adding to their existing sociocultural identities. At the same time, through their participation, our classroom communities also change to include new ways of think-ing and behaving; both the member and the community change and grow in their sense of identity. For this to happen effectively, you and the entire school will need to consciously support and draw on the sociocultural knowledge and experiences that immigrant English learners bring to your classrooms and school community. In later chapters, we show how teachers and school communities support immigrant students' sociocultural identities as the students gain a sense of who they can become and the futures that are available to them.

5. *Wider community contexts are tied into and built upon, as English learners become participants in questioning and redesigning local contexts and beyond* (CONNECTIONS TO WIDER CONTEXTS). Social justice issues that question and address social stratification, exclusionary practices, and societal racism can and should be addressed in the classroom. This commitment falls under the idea that students can learn to use language to critique what seems normal and natural as well as to create alternative, more just social worlds (Janks, 1993; Oakes & Rogers, 2006). Approaches for promoting critical con-sciousness within the classroom and school communities can facili-tate language and academic learning while addressing inequitable distribution of power and other issues of social justice. In later chapters, we point out ways for you to create spaces for conversa-tions about social justice issues, to invite students to question every-day texts about the world in which we live, and to involve students in community action projects (Leland & Harste, 2004; Oakes & Rogers, 2006; Shannon, 1995). Issues of social justice reside in the

communities we inhabit with our students, and so these issues can become a part of the discussions and activities our communities engage in, including those of academic learning communities. While students engage in wider communities, their sense of identity within those communities also grows.

Main Ideas in Review

Here are the commitments in practice that frame and guide what you plan and carry out in your classroom to ensure access, participation, meaning making, identity formation, and critical awareness and transformation.

1. ACTIVE PARTICIPATION
2. SOCIAL INTEGRATION
3. INTEGRATED LANGUAGE LEARNING
4. SOCIOCULTURAL IDENTITY SUPPORT
5. CONNECTIONS TO WIDER CONTEXTS

As we build on these commitments by showing how you can incorporate them into your practices, we realize that these are only the tips of what is possible for how the particular sets of community practices in your classrooms might evolve and improve. In the following sections, we discuss some of the other issues and practices that you will need to learn about as you begin to plan for and put into action your commitments in practice.

TEACHING IN THE PRESENT POLITICAL CLIMATE

These are difficult times for many teachers (Poynor & Wolfe, 2005). The current political climate has taken the notion of accountability to the ultima Thule. The No Child Left Behind Act (2001) mandates that all students be tested numerous times from 1st through 12th grades. Nearly half of states nationwide have legislated high-stakes high school exit exams. Teachers not only have to teach English learners academic content and language, but now also have to prepare them for these standardized tests. Schools are threatened with state takeover if the test scores fall below a certain point. This threat puts an immense amount of stress on teachers, especially teachers of students who will be tested on content in their target language.

How can secondary teachers of English learners help prepare these students for the tests? First, we believe that teachers who focus on the commitments in practice are, in effect, preparing students for tests. The best way to prepare students for the tests (and for life) is to facilitate active learning within academic discourses. Second, many teachers have found it helpful to teach test-taking skills along with academic content. English learners may not be privy to specific expectations and discourses around standardized tests, so these need to be made explicit to your students. Providing English learners with practice tests and tips on and strategies for answering questions (process of elimination, bubbling correctly, skipping unknown questions and coming back to them) can increase test scores. You can include these test-taking preparations without taking an excessive amount of time from academic learning. We do not believe academic curriculum should be designed for high test scores, in other words, teaching to the test. Our students have strengths and needs far beyond what can be contained in a singular, standardized assessment.

You can also use standardized tests as an opportunity for critical discussions about the history, design, and purposes of tests in school with respect to socially stratifying students according to test scores (see Christensen, 2000; Oakes & Rogers, 2006, the Futures Project). You can have students examine different types of standardized tests and discuss the discursive properties of questions, to uncover how the tests themselves privilege certain knowledge and ways of showing knowledge. You might also invite students to create test questions of their own, in their own dialects or languages, and based on their own cultures, using comparisons, vocabulary, and the like that students outside of their cultural experiences would not have experience with. In this way, the students critically contextualize standardized tests socioculturally and historically while learning about discursive features in the actual questions.

ADDRESSING DISTRICT AND STATE STANDARDS

In addition to preparing for standardized tests, secondary teachers of English learners are held responsible for district and state standards. In most states, academic standards are relatively general. Although the standards dictate *what* must be covered, they do not usually dictate *how* they must be covered. For example, if high school history standards dictate that the Revolutionary War must be covered, they do not usually specify that students must read Chapter 6 on the Revolution and answer the questions at the end of the chapter. You can have students do individual or small group projects on some aspect of the times during the Revolution from people to battles to art to science. You can have students study revolutions as a thematic unit and compare the U.S. Revolution with others in history (or in present times). You can draw from student interests and backgrounds to make content-related decisions that will "cover" the standards while also fitting students' needs for relevance, interest, and a place in the curriculum. All five commitments in practice can be addressed within any state or district standard we have seen thus far.

Because these are high-stakes times in education, you must be aware of state and district standards and look at what ways your teaching meets the standards. Good teaching should dictate how standards are met and not the other way around.

One mistake some secondary teachers have made over the years has been to focus on a standardized curriculum without any regard to who the students are who populate their classrooms. Secondary teachers have relied on what Paulo Freire (1970) calls the banking model of teaching. In this approach, the teacher's main responsibility is to transmit knowledge to the empty heads of students. The problem with this model is that it positions learners as passive recipients, and it matters not whether what they are being taught is relevant to their lives. In this book, we encourage a way of teaching based on commitments in practice that is the polar opposite of the banking model. We advocate active participation, choice, building on what students bring to your classes, social responsibility, and interactive language acquisition.

DISTINGUISHING BETWEEN CONTEXT AND "REMEDIAL" INSTRUCTION

A common misconception is that sheltered content classes or methods for teaching English learners are remedial in form. This is far from the truth, and a somewhat troubling concept if you consider that the implications are that English learners have learning disabilities because they don't speak English. By extension, teachers of mainstream students sometimes express concern that the changes they need to make in their teaching will "dumb down" instruction. However, contextualized instruction that supports all learners is not remedialized instruction. An example might be found in chemistry. Students who take part in an experiment in a science lab are taking part in contextualized instruction. On the other hand, students who read about the experiment in a textbook are "covering" the same material, but it is devoid of context. The material is the same, but the hands-on experimentation helps provide contextual support for English learners. All learners need rigor and relevance in instruction. Adding context to content does not dumb it down, but it does make it more accessible to all learners.

Competition is rampant in schools (Kozol, 2005). Students compete in sports, compete for grades, and compete for grades in classroom activities. In the meantime, sociocultural learning theories inform us that learning is best facilitated inside supportive learning communities. This entails another switch in thinking for teachers. Instead of initiating activities that are based entirely in competition, teachers must initiate activities that build community. Community can be built around the practice of science and social studies and the like in a way that ensures rigorous learning. Moreover, building community can accomplish this without marginalizing or excluding anyone.

In the next chapter, we introduce you to Newcomer Centers and how your secondary school can use this support structure to prepare immigrant English learners for your classrooms, so that when they come to your classrooms they are relatively adjusted to English and how U.S. secondary schools operate.

Summary

This chapter presented the organizing principles for teaching immigrant and English learners in academic content classes using commitments in practice, which are defined and explained in some detail. It is important to become familiar with the five commitments in practice so that you can see how they are integrated into the academic content vignettes in later chapters. Here are some of the main ideas discussed in this chapter:

- Secondary teachers who work well with immigrant students and English learners have commitments in practice to guide them in planning and carrying out their daily activities.
- Successful secondary students become members of academic communities of practice.
- Membership in academic communities of practice requires students to use language, think, act, and behave in ways that are

recognized and valued by people who are already members of the academic community of practice.

- Identity formation and affiliation are important parts of gaining membership in academic communities of practice.
- Learning to use commitments in practice to plan and organize your classroom takes time and effort, especially in times of demand for high accountability and high-stakes testing, both of which undermine creative teaching and teaching that pays attention to tracking, social stratification, and other social injustices.

We urge you to spend considerable time studying these commitments in practice so that you can both recognize and use them in your teaching experiences. Just as you identify yourself as a specific content area teacher (and member of that community), you want your students to create and affiliate with identities that also provide access to the practices that enable them to show membership through talk, participation, and use of materials that are necessary to the community of practice.

References

Block, D. (2003). *The social turn in second language acquisition*. Washington, DC: Georgetown University Press.

Christensen, L. (2000). *Reading, writing, and rising up*. Milwaukee, WI: Rethinking Schools.

Cohen, E. (1994). *Designing groupwork: Strategies for the heterogeneous classroom*. New York: Teachers College Press.

Cummins, J. (1979). Linguistic interdependence and the educational development of bilingual children. *Review of Educational Research, 49*, 222–251.

Edelsky, C. (1994). Education for democracy. *Language Arts, 71*, 252–257.

Edelsky, C. (2006). *With literacy and justice for all: Rethinking the social in language and education* (4th ed.). Mahwah, NJ: Lawrence Erlbaum Associates.

Edelsky, C., Smith, K., & Wolfe, P. (2002). A discourse on academic discourse. *Linguistics and Education, 13*(1), 1–38.

Freire, P. (1970). *Pedagogy of the oppressed*. New York: Seabury Press.

Gee, J. (2004). *Situated language and learning: A critique of traditional schools*. New York: Routledge.

Halliday, M. A. K. (1975). *Learning how to mean: Explorations in the development of language*. London: Arnold.

Hawkins, M. (2004). Researching English language and literacy development in schools. *Educational Researcher, 33*(3), 14–25.

Janks, H. (1993). *Language, identity and power*. Johannesburg, South Africa: Hodder.

Kanno, Y., & Applebaum, S. (1995). ESL students speak up: Stories of how we are doing. *TESL Canada Journal, 12*(2), 32–49.

Kanno, Y., & Norton, B. (2003). Imagined communities and educational possibilities: Introduction. *Journal of Language, Identity, and Education, 2*(4), 241–249.

Kozol, J. (2005). *Shame on the nation: The restoration of apartheid schooling in America.* New York: Crown Publishing.

Krashen, S. (1982). *Principles and practice in second language acquisition.* New York: Pergamon Press.

Lave, J., & Wenger, E. (1991). *Situated learning: Legitimate peripheral participation.* New York: Cambridge University Press.

Leland, C., & Harste, J. (2004). Critical literacy: Enlarging the space of the possible. In V. Vásquez, K. Egawa, J. Harste, & R. Thompson (Eds.), *Literacy as social practice* (pp. 129–135). Urbana, IL: National Council of Teachers of English.

Lemke, J. (1990). *Talking science: Language, learning and values.* Norwood, NJ: Ablex.

MacSwan, J. (2000). The threshold hypothesis, semilingualism and other contributions to a deficit view of linguistic minorities. *Hispanic Journal of Behavior Sciences, 22,* 3–45.

Matuti-Bianchi, M. G. (1986). Ethnic identities and patterns of school success and failure among Mexican-descent and Japanese American students in a California high school. *American Journal of Education, 95,* 233–255.

Minicucci, C., & Olsen, L. (1992). *Programs for secondary limited English proficient students: A California study.* Washington, DC: National Clearinghouse for Bilingual Education.

Norton, B. (2000). *Identity and language learning: Gender, ethnicity and educational change.* Essex, England: Pearson Education.

Oakes, J., & Rogers, J. (2006). *Learning power: Organizing for education and justice.* New York: Teachers College Press.

Olsen, L. (1997). *Made in America: Immigrant students in our public schools.* New York: The New Press.

Olsen, L., & Jaramillo, A. (1999). *Turning the tides of exclusion: A guide for educators and advocates for immigrant students.* Oakland, CA: California Tomorrow.

Ruíz-de-Velasco, J., & Fix, M. (2000). *Overlooked & underserved: Immigrant students in U.S. secondary schools.* New York: The Urban Institute.

Shannon, P. (1995). *Text, lies, and videotape.* Portsmouth, NH: Heinemann.

Suárez-Orozco, C. (2005). Identities under siege: Immigration stress and social mirroring among children of immigrants. In M. Suárez-Orozco, C. Suárez-Orozco, & D. Qin-Hillard (Eds.), *The new immigration: An interdisciplinary reader* (pp. 135–156). New York: Routledge.

Suárez-Orozco, C., & Todorova, I. (2003, Winter). The social worlds of immigrant youth. *New Directions for Youth Development,* 15–25.

Suárez-Orozco, M.(2005). Everything you ever wanted to know about assimilation but were afraid to ask. In M. Suárez-Orozco, C. Suárez-Orozco, & D. Qin-Hillard, (Eds.), *The new immigration: An interdisciplinary reader* (pp. 67–84). New York: Routledge.

Toohey, K. (2000). *Learning English at school: Identity, social relations and classroom practice.* Clevedon, England: Multilingual Matters, Ltd.

Valdés, G. (2001). *Learning and not learning English: Latino students in American schools.* New York: Teachers College Press.

Vygotsky, L. S. (1978). *Mind in society.* Cambridge, MA: Harvard University Press.

Watson-Gegeo, K. (2004). Mind, language, and epistemology: Toward a language socialization paradigm for SLA. *Modern Language Journal, 88*(3), 331–350.

Wenger, E. (1998). *Communities of practice: Learning, meaning and identity.* New York: Cambridge University Press.

Wolfe, P. (2004). "The Owl Cried"; Reading abstract literary concepts with adolescent ESL students. *Journal of Adolescent and Adult Literacy, 47*(5), 402–413.

Wolfe, P., & Faltis, C. (1999). Gender and ideology in secondary ESL and bilingual classrooms. In C. Faltis & P. Wolfe (Eds.), *So much to say: Adolescents, bilingualism, & ESL in the secondary school* (pp. 84–104). New York: Teachers College Press.

Newcomer Centers and Programs for Immigrant Students

Rebert Pham/PH College

OVERVIEW

In this chapter, we familiarize you with programs and practices for recently arriving immigrant students, which include *refugees* (immigrants who come to the United States for political asylum or to escape political persecution). You will learn about newcomer centers and programs, what they can offer immigrant students, and how you can provide them support for their efforts to prepare immigrant students for your classrooms. Newcomer centers and programs are temporary transitional sets of experiences designed to meet the unique needs of newcomer immigrant students in a nurturing and supportive educational environment. Newcomer centers and programs prepare newly arrived immigrants with an orientation to school, a specialized curriculum, and access to a wide variety of support services.

We begin with a discussion of the kinds of immigrant students that you will likely be teaching and learning about and from. Knowing about the kinds of social and educational experiences of the immigrant students who are likely to attend your school will help you offer the best attention to their particular needs. Following this, we provide descriptions of newcomer centers and programs, with sections on program types, curricular options, transitions, and commitments in practice. The guiding questions for this chapter are:

- What kinds of immigrant students enroll in secondary schools nationwide? How do their language and academic needs vary?
- Given the variation among immigrant students, what kinds of newcomer support services are offered for all students, and what kinds of special services are offered for students who are least familiar with U.S. schools?
- What do secondary newcomer centers and programs look like? What are some of the benefits and drawbacks of separate newcomer centers and programs?
- How do newcomer students make the transition from newcomer centers and programs to your classrooms?
- What can you do to facilitate the transition so that newcomer students are welcomed in your classrooms?

NEWCOMER IMMIGRANT STUDENTS: THE BIG PICTURE

Imagine what it must be like to come to the United States and enroll in secondary school not knowing English or how the school works. You would not only be unable to participate in class, but also be a stranger in a strange land. If you came from a world where the majority of people are extremely poor and undernourished, where children regularly beg for food, where school is only for boys, where no one else in your family has gone past the sixth grade, where books are a luxury costing more than you earn in a week, landing in high school in America could be a daunting experience for you. You could come as a refugee from Somalia, Bosnia, Iraq, or the Sudan. You could be from Haiti, India, the Philippines, or the Ukraine. You could speak Albanian, Bengali, Chinese, Kurdish, Polish, Punjabi, Swahili, or Thai.

Most likely, however, you would speak Spanish (or an indigenous language such as Náhuatl, Maya, Zapoteco, Mixteco, Otomí, or one of 55 others) and come from Mexico or Central America, the places of origin of at least one of the parents of more than 65% of all recent immigrants in the last decade (Jamieson, Curry, & Martínez, 2001). In 2001, 9.6% of all school-aged children learning English were immigrants or children of immigrants, and 75% of the more than 4.5 million English learners enrolled in language support programs, such as bilingual and English-as-a-second-language classes, were Spanish speakers. Nearly a million and a half English learners were enrolled in secondary school (grades 7–12), and 79% came from Spanish-speaking countries (Kindler, 2002; Ruíz-de-Velasco & Fix, 2000).

When you moved to the United States, you would also likely live in a neighborhood populated by members of your ethnic and language group. In this neighborhood, you would have little or no contact with English speakers from the mainstream middle class. McDonnell and Hill (1993) note that 78% of the newly arrived immigrants locate in the largest cities in California, Texas, New York, Florida, and Illinois. Moreover, nearly 80% of immigrant students residing in these states attend predominantly minority schools (Frankenberg, Lee, & Orfield, 2003).

If you were from Mexico or Central America, by far the most populous group of immigrant students to have entered the United States in recent years (McArthur 1993; Kindler, 2002), you would belong to America's most segregated minority group. The average Latino immigrant student attends a school that is less than 30% White, where a majority of the students are poor and in the process of learning English as a second language. Latino immigrant English learners attend school where over 60% of the students are Latino (Orfield, Frankenberg, & Lee, 2002). By comparison, if you were an immigrant English learner from an Asian country, you would likely attend a school where only one quarter of the student body is Asian.

■ **Reflection**
Interview a first-generation immigrant who came to America prior to 1950. Ask him or her about the following: reasons for coming to America, views about becoming American, and experiences in school. Then, compare and contrast what you learn with the experiences of recent immigrants to America.

If you were poor in your home country, you would likely live in a poor neighborhood and be consistently exposed to gang activity and violence (Olsen, 1997; Walqui, 2000). Your family would shop, conduct business, and have personal networks of friends and acquaintances within this neighborhood, which forms community funds of knowledge (Moll & González, 2004). You and your family would be less likely to receive health care, making fewer doctor and dental visits for routine checkups, taking less medication, and making fewer trips to the emergency room (Connolly, 2005). One of the reasons for this is that in immigrant neighborhoods, there are fewer nearby hospitals, clinics, physicians, dentists, and pharmacies.

VARIATION AMONG IMMIGRANT STUDENTS

Many immigrant students arrive in high school not knowing English. As we have outlined above, not knowing English may be the least of the challenges many immigrant adolescents face when they enroll in high school. In this section, we discuss the variation among immigrant adolescents based on the extent and quality of prior formal schooling experiences they had in their home country and in the United States prior to reaching high school. We also bring into the discussion how easy or difficult their transition to the United States may have been as well as how similarities and differences between their home country and the United States may have an impact on their adjustment and, ultimately, their achievement in school.

Parallel Formal Schooling

Let's begin by thinking of adolescent immigrants in terms of a skewed hourglass (Suárez-Orozco, 2005): At the top you have immigrants who enter secondary school in the United States with parallel formal schooling experiences. These students account for about a third of all adolescent immigrants. By *parallel*, we mean that these immigrant students have attended formal schooling up to the grade level at which they enter U.S. schools. These students are typically highly literate in their home language and are highly proficient in technology, including computer technology, cell phone texting, and transglobal Internet uses. Oftentimes, immigrant students with parallel formal schooling have also studied English, along with one or more other languages of wider communication. Depending on their family resources, they may have even attended private bilingual schools and traveled extensively to English-speaking countries before immigrating to the United States. The parents of these students are well educated, and many either come to the United States for advanced degrees or already have them when they move to the United States. Parenthetically, many of the Nobel prize winners from the United States have been first-generation immigrants, most with parallel (or better) formal education upon arrival to the United States.

Non-Parallel Formal Schooling

At the other, base end of the hourglass are large numbers of adolescent newly arrived immigrants with non-parallel formal schooling experiences. By *non-parallel*, we mean that these immigrant students have sporadic formal schooling experiences and are typically underschooled—two or more grades behind where they would be if they had not had interrupted schooling in their home country. These students are likely not to be technologically proficient with computers, and their literacy practices vary greatly from those of most immigrants with parallel schooling experiences. Ruiz-de-Velasco and Fix (2000), for example, found that 32% of English learners in secondary school across the nation had missed 2 or more years of schooling since age 6. Among immigrant adolescents aged 15 to 17 from Latin American countries, more than one third were enrolled below grade level in U.S. schools (Jamieson et al., 2001).

There are two things to clarify about this hourglass metaphor: One, the middle area is substantially smaller than the two ends. That is, adolescent immigrants in the past 25 years have tended to belong either to the wealthier, privileged, educated classes of their home country (the upper portion of the hourglass) or they belong to the working class or poorer (the lower portion of the hourglass). Although adolescent immigrants belonging to the middle class come to the United States (for example, from Korea, the Philippines, and Taiwan), their numbers are significantly smaller compared to the other two groups. Two, the overwhelming majority of adolescent immigrants come from conditions of poverty, and they continue to live in poverty in the United States, often for generations (Portes & Macloud, 2005). (See Table 3.1 for a summary of newcomer students.)

Table 3.1
Parallel and Non-Parallel Newcomer Students

Parallel Newcomers	Non-Parallel Newcomers
Formal schooling at least equal to the grade level they enter	Formal schooling several grade levels below the grade level they enter
Computer literate and technologically experienced	Little or no knowledge of or experience with computer technology
Familiar with routines, practices, and appropriate behavior in school	May be unfamiliar with how school works, what services are available, daily routines, and classroom behavior
May have some experience with English, usually English grammar, not conversational English	May have little or no experience learning English
Transition to U.S. school may be smooth	Transition to U.S. school may be traumatic and difficult with support services

Long-Term English Learners

In addition to parallel and non-parallel immigrant students, there is a third type of immigrant student that shows up in U.S. high schools: long-term English learners (Minicucci & Olsen, 1992). These are students who arrived in the United States as young children and have had either insufficient language or academic support or they participated in limited English-as-a-second-language preparation programs. These students continue into secondary schools with insufficient academic English fluency and academic content knowledge to benefit fully from being mainstreamed into all-English classes. They are often referred to as *Generation 1.5s* or more disparagingly as *English as a second language (ESL) lifers.* Like immigrant students with non-parallel formal schooling, long-term English learners have gaps in academic content knowledge and may have had difficulties becoming academically literate in English. Unlike non-parallel immigrants, however, these students are usually proficient in conversational English and familiar with schooling routines and classroom practices and, therefore, will not be placed in newcomer centers or programs when they arrive in high school.

One other way to distinguish newly arrived adolescent immigrants is on the basis of the belief systems they use to guide them in their understanding of how larger society works for or against them and of their place as new immigrants within school and in that larger society (Ogbu, 1991). Immigrants who move to the United States with the

■ **Reflection**

Does it matter for you as a teacher to know about the formal educational experiences of the immigrant students that you might have in class? Why or why not?

belief that they will gain better educational and economic opportunities tend to interpret any economic, political, and social barriers they came up against in school or society as temporary, as problems they will or can overcome with the passage of time, hard work, and more education. Some adolescent immigrant students holding this belief of optimism also see that their present situation is a vast improvement over their former situation back home. These students have a dual frame of reference where they compare what they have now with that was available to them in their home country. Immigrant students who subscribe to this belief system have a strong incentive to succeed in school, even when severe gaps in knowledge make high school seem like an insurmountable challenge.

In a similar vein, adolescent immigrants who arrive in U.S. high schools with the belief that their educational experiences went well beyond what U.S. schools offer may have a difficult transition. These students with parallel schooling experiences may even do poorly in some of the academic materials they are required to take (Phelan, Davidson, & Yu, 1998).

NEWCOMER SCHOOLS AND PROGRAMS

The idea that newly arrived adolescent immigrants could benefit from sets of experiences to help them become familiar with U.S. schools and to prepare them for the kinds of language and literacy they will need to be successful in school was first launched in the late 1970s. Since then, when only 4 newcomer programs existed, more than 115 secondary newcomer programs have been documented in more than 29 states and the District of Columbia (Boyson & Short, 2003).

One of the reasons for the increase in newcomer schools and programs is that existing programs, such as English-as-a-second-language and bilingual programs, are only effective when the students in them have literacy abilities and are familiar with the way American schools operate. As we pointed out above, many adolescent immigrants enter secondary school with gaps in their literacy abilities and may also be unfamiliar with formal schooling. Newcomer schools and programs can provide such students with a safe environment to meet the needs of older students, especially when they do not have to compete with students who are already literate and accustomed to secondary school life.

Newcomer Program Types

There are three types of newcomer programs: Programs within a school, a separate program at a separate site, and a whole school. The most common type of newcomer program is housed within the school building, where newly arrived immigrant students have opportunities to interact with English speakers at least part of the day in nonacademic classes such as physical education, music, and art. Newcomer students may attend programs within a school for one or two class periods, for a half day, or for a whole day. The length of the program depends on resources available and the special needs of the immigrant students being served. Most newcomer programs within schools are a half day or a full day. Students in these programs typically stay in them up to a full year, with more time made available as needed.

Some school districts opt for a separate location to house the newcomer program, especially to serve students from more than one school. Separate newcomer programs are usually for the whole school day, unless the school district can provide bus transportation to and from the students' designated home schools. Most students who attend separate newcomer programs stay approximately one year.

The least common type of program is when an entire school is designed for newly arrived immigrants. The most well-known immigrant school is International High School in New York (Ancess, 2003). This school accepts only recently arrived immigrants with non-parallel formal schooling experiences. There are only six newcomer high schools nationwide. Students in newcomer high schools may remain in the program for as long as it takes them to graduate or until they reach age 21.

The Benefits of Separate Newcomer Programs

The idea of having separate newcomer programs where students are segregated from the mainstream student population for some or all of the day for an extended period is anathema to some educators. Separate programs conjure up notions of inferior education (from the separate but equal days) and apartheid (a policy of separation based on racial discrimination). However, the use of separate programs for newcomers does not necessarily have to be detrimental to adolescent English learners the way it is and has been for native English-speaking students who are ethnically distinct, such as African Americans, Chicanos, Puerto Ricans, and Native Americans. There are some benefits to segregating immigrant English learners from all-English classrooms while they are acquiring English and becoming familiar with American school routines and practices. Three of the main benefits are:

1. *Greater participation.* When newly arrived students don't have to compete with native English speakers, they can participate more fully in learning English. English instruction for newly arrived immigrants provides a safe environment for learning.

2. *Cultural sensitivity.* Teachers who work in newcomer centers are generally more sensitive to students' language and school cultural needs. These teachers usually have more experience and preparation in working with English learners than do content area secondary teachers.

3. *Collective sense of belonging.* Separate programs enable immigrant students to develop a collective sense of belonging to the school in a family-like atmosphere. Students who study and learn together, and who experience the same difficulties in school due to language and cultural differences, tend to develop a bond that intimately connects them to their school program.

Some Drawbacks to Separating Newcomer Students

Although there are some advantages to separating immigrant newcomers to ensure they participate in and benefit from classroom learning experiences, keeping them apart from native English speakers can also be detrimental (Feinberg, 2000). Four issues to consider are:

1. *Linguistic isolation.* Separating newcomer students from native English speakers can deny them access to conversation and other language-related forms of interaction that are necessary to gain high levels of English proficiency. Linguistic isolation is most likely to be an issue for students who have gained conversational proficiency in English.

2. *Social isolation.* The social segregation of minority students along class and ethnic lines is already a problem in many schools. Nearly all English learners are also members of minority groups who experience social isolation. Students cannot learn about or from one another, which can contribute to and reinforce negative stereotypes.

3. *Labeling.* Immigrant students who are placed into newcomer centers and programs for long periods are often labeled as monolinguals,

LEPS (limited-English-proficient students), and other terms that denote some kind of language limitation. The meanings of these labels may be extended to infer some kind of intellectual inferiority or learning disability. Moreover, when students are referred to by these labels, their identity as individual students may be minimized.

4. *Separate but unequal.* Separate newcomer classes and programs for immigrant English learners may not be equal to regular classes and programs in terms of the materials and preparation of the teachers who work in them. One study of newcomer centers (Constantino & Lavandez, 1993) found that English instruction was little more than pattern-practice drillwork, coupled with memorization and other rote work. Teacher education to prepare high school ESL and newcomer center teachers is unavailable nationwide. In some cases, high school level English-as-a-second-language teachers are either self-taught or inadequately prepared to teach students with non-parallel schooling experiences (García, 1999).

A key to having a successful program especially for newcomer immigrant students is to pay attention to the possible shortcomings by performing formative and summative evaluations with these issues in mind.

NEWCOMER CURRICULAR OPTIONS

Course offerings vary depending on whether newcomer centers and programs operate at a separate site or on campus, and whether they run on a full-time or part-time basis. However, regardless of the type of program, all offer immigrant students English-as-a-second-language or English language development courses (Boyson & Short, 2003; Chang, 1990; Friedlander, 1991). Students initially focus on oral proficiency to develop written English proficiency. In most cases, students study English at one of four levels: beginning, intermediate, advanced, and transitional. These classes prepare students in conversational as well as academic oral and written English, depending on their primary language literacy abilities (Short, 1998).

Some newcomer programs incorporate sheltered content instruction, which teaches English in tandem with academic content. *Sheltered content instruction* (Krashen, 1985) is a way of teaching academic content to English learners by adjusting interaction to make it comprehensible through a variety of strategies such as modeling, scaffolding, hands-on activities, visual support, graphic organizers, and realia (real-life objects and artifacts). The goal is accessibility for English learners to content area concepts while they continue to improve their oral and written English proficiency (Echevarria & Graves, 2003; see also Faltis, 1993).

Since many newcomer students arrive with non-parallel schooling experiences, they may also receive literacy instruction in the primary language while they are learning English. For these students learning to read and write in a language they already understand and use to make meaning is the best way to introduce and develop literacy quickly (Pérez, 2004).

Newly arrived immigrant students, parallel and non-parallel alike, will also receive information about the routines, school policies and procedures, and classroom behaviors that most American students take for granted. Table 3.2 gives a list of some of the topics that newly arrived immigrant students need to know about to be able to function safely and appropriately in secondary school. How much time and effort is spent on these topics depends on a student's experiences with formal schooling and American schools.

Table 3.2
What Newly Arrived Immigrants Need to Know About School Routines and Practices

During School Hours	After School Hours
School passes and how to use them (including tardy and detention slips)	The nature of parent conferences and attendance
How the cafeteria works: Line formation, lunch passes	Parent Teacher Organizations
Fire drills and exit plans	School dances, proms, special events
Assemblies, pep rallies, awards, and award ceremonies	Field days, types of permission required
Holidays, festivities, and traditional celebrations	After-school and Saturday tutoring programs
Fund raisers	Clubs, honor societies, sports activities
Health examinations and screening for vision and hearing	How detention and suspension work
What in-school suspension means; disciplinary methods	Summer school options
Guidance counseling for course selection and college	Extracurricular activities such as sports (competitive level in high school, not necessarily for beginners)
How to qualify for free lunch	
Sex education and physical education	

TRANSITIONS TO REGULAR CLASSROOM AND SCHOOL SETTINGS

Making the transition from a newcomer center or program to classrooms that are geared for native English-speaking students can be either smooth or difficult, depending on how much planning for the transition has been done before a student is exited from the program. A good newcomer program will engage in ongoing discussions with the staff and teachers who will receive the newcomer students when they exit (Boyson & Short, 2003). Likewise, the newcomer students will make several visits to the school and meet with teachers and guidance counselors to make the transition as smooth, accommodating, and inviting as possible. In these visits, the newcomer students should learn about class and lunch schedules; the locations of the classrooms, library, and bathrooms; the kinds of extracurricular clubs and sports programs that are available; and the kinds of classroom study materials and books required for each of their classes.

Once the newcomer students are placed in their classrooms, the school needs to monitor their progress in English language development and academic content learning. Just as importantly, the school should also be in close contact with the teachers who have newcomer students to offer them opportunities to participate in staff development activities related to teaching adolescent English learners. Oftentimes, these teachers have bilingual paraprofessionals to assist them throughout the day. Paraprofessionals should also be encouraged to participate in English-learner-related staff development activities (Short, 1998).

■ **Reflection**

What does your high school already do to facilitate immigrant students' transitions from newcomer centers and programs to your school? What recommendations would you make to improve the transition and to provide ongoing support services to newcomer students in your classes?

Most newcomer centers and programs provide family-oriented events and activities designed to acclimate newcomer families to the school and community (Boyson & Short, 2003). In addition to helping newcomer students with social and health services, newcomer centers and programs use bilingual community workers and school liaisons to reach out to families in these critical areas. A majority of newcomer centers and programs offer adult-level English-as-a-second-language classes either at the newcomer school site or at a nearby location within the school district boundaries. Typically these ESL classes also provide parents with an orientation to school routines, policies, and practices, along with information about American society (Chang, 1990). Increasingly, high school districts with large numbers of immigrant students are beginning to offer parenting programs, GED courses in Spanish, citizenship classes, employment services, and career education (Boyson & Short, 2003).

COMMITMENTS IN PRACTICE

We conclude this chapter with a short discussion on how the five commitments in practice can be applied to newcomer centers and programs. Second language acquisition for both parallel and non-parallel immigrant English learners requires active participation in activities that foster oral and written language growth. For immigrant students who are new to American schools, the practice of social interaction in whole and small groups may require preparation through team building and other kinds of structured learning strategies. In many countries throughout the world, students are taught to listen to their teachers and not to ask questions or to speak out. Students with this approach to learning will need to be shown how to participate appropriately, how to get the floor by bidding (raising hands), and how to take turns in small group work in which conversation is crucial for learning.

Immigrant students who are new to English should not be placed in classroom settings where they would need to compete with fully fluent English speakers. Nonetheless, beginning English learners can and should be integrated socially and physically with other English learners of various levels of proficiency. Heterogeneous social integration (Commitment in Practice #2) within all classes (English, academic subjects, literacy, and about American schools and society) fosters language acquisition because students will need to negotiate meaning with their classmates. The negotiation of meaning necessarily invites learners to clarify, to use their developing English, and to confirm understanding about a wide range of topics (Commitment in Practice #3). Even in classes that focus primarily on learning about English (English grammar, spelling, morphology, writing mechanics, etc.), opportunities abound for students to exchange ideas and use their developing English with their peers of differing language proficiency levels.

Newcomers who learn English in preparation for their academic courses in school need ample experiences to make meaning with, learn about, and learn through English while they are actively participating (Commitment in Practice #1) in practices valued and reinforced in their newcomer classes. In this manner, in the process of being acquired into conversational and academic varieties of English, students also acquire the means to participate appropriately and actively in academic classrooms.

Newcomer centers and programs should be places where immigrant students can feel safe to rely on their sociocultural identities (Commitment in Practice #4) while they add on new identities as

English learners and members of the school communities of practice. Having staff (teachers, paraprofessionals, liaisons, counselors, and administration) who are sensitive to the language and cultural affinities that immigrant students bring with them to newcomer centers and programs is critical for helping students gain a collective sense of belonging as they become attuned to English and adjusted to the school.

Finally, students in newcomer centers and programs need to see that what they are accomplishing in school is connected to wider issues in the world that surround them (Commitment in Practice #5). Students should be prepared for the kinds of social stratification that happens in high school (through tracking) and society, and be given the tools to navigate the system to their benefit. They need to know how to work with guidance counselors to get the courses they need to graduate. They should learn about learning strategies to help them learn specialized vocabulary and how to take standardized tests, and what their rights are with respect to standardized test-taking procedures. They can learn about ways to address peer group pressures and how to handle name calling and bullying.

> ■ **Reflection**
> Think about the kinds of knowledge and support you would want if you were suddenly uprooted and had to attend high school in a completely foreign environment. Would you want to first attend a newcomer center, or would you prefer to enroll immediately in school? Why or why not?

CONCLUSION

In the following chapters, we present scenarios of academic classrooms in which immigrant students are actively participating as they learn English and are acquired into the academic community of practice aligned with the content area. For each of the academic content areas (language arts, science, history, and mathematics), we show how commitments in practice support immigrant students as they acquire English, engage in practices, and gain affinities for the social and academic ways of being, doing, and believing that members of real and imagined communities recognize, value, and use.

Summary

Many students who enter secondary school are newcomers, immigrant students who are unfamiliar with American school systems, rules, and manners of participation. Others are students who are continuing from elementary and middle school, and some are still learning English. Among newcomers, some students have had parallel schooling, whereas others have gaps in their learning, which we refer to as non-parallel schooling experiences. Newcomer centers and programs offer both types of newcomers a way to adjust to secondary school and to become attuned to English, in preparation for all-English content classes. The following ideas are a summary of what this chapter presents:

- There are various types of newcomer centers and programs, each having benefits and drawbacks.
- Most newcomer centers keep students one year or less.
- Non-parallel newcomers have different learning needs from newcomers with parallel schooling in the home country.
- All newcomers need to learn about rules, routines, safety concerns, and available school programs.
- Once newcomers transition to all-English classrooms, they may need continued support services and monitoring for success.

Even though you might not be directly involved in teaching newcomer immigrants and students who are new to English, it is important to support efforts to provide these students with the best education possible. When these students progress to all-English classes, you are there to support them, using your commitments in practice to facilitate their participation and ultimately, their academic achievement.

References

Ancess, J. (2003). *Beating the odds: High schools as communities of commitment.* New York: Teachers College Press.

Boyson, B., & Short, D. (2003). *Secondary school newcomer programs in the United States.* Santa Cruz, CA: Center for Research on Education, Diversity & Excellence.

Chang, H. N. (1990). *Newcomer programs: Innovative efforts to meet the educational challenges of immigrant students.* San Francisco: California Tomorrow.

Connolly, C. (2005, July 27). Immigrants' health care falls short, study finds. *The Arizona Republic,* p. A16.

Constantino, R., & Lavandez, M. (1993). Newcomer schools: First impressions. *Peabody Journal of Education, 69*(1), 82–101.

Echevarria, J., & Graves, A. (2003). *Sheltered content instruction: Teaching English language learners with diverse abilities.* Boston, MA: Allyn & Bacon.

Faltis, C. (1993). Critical issues in the use of sheltered content teaching in high school bilingual programs. *Peabody Journal of Education, 69*(1), 136–150.

Feinberg, R. (2000). Newcomer school: Salvation or segregated oblivion for immigrant students. *Theory into Practice, 39*(4), 220–227.

Frankenberg, E., Lee, C., & Orfield, G. (2003). *A multiracial society with segregated schools: Are we losing the dream?* Cambridge, MA: The Civil Rights Project, Harvard University.

Friedlander, M. (1991). *The newcomer program: Helping immigrant students succeed in U.S. schools.* Washington, DC: National Clearinghouse for Bilingual Education.

García, O. (1999). Educating Latino high school students with little formal schooling. In C. Faltis & P. Wolfe (Eds.), *So much to say: Adolescents, bilingualism, and ESL in the secondary school* (pp. 61–82). New York: Teachers College Press.

Jamieson, A., Curry, A., & Martínez, G. (2001). School enrollment in the United States—Social and economic characteristics of students. *Current Population Reports, P20–533.* Washington, DC: U.S. Government Printing Office.

Kindler, A. (2002). *Survey of states' limited English proficient students and available educational programs and services, 2000–2007: Summary report.* Washington DC: National Clearinghouse for English Language Acquisition.

Krashen, S. (1985). *The input hypothesis: Issues and implications.* New York: Longman.

McArthur, E. (1993). *Language characteristics and schooling in the United States: A changing picture, 1979 and 1989.* Washington, DC: U.S. Department of Education.

McDonnell, L., & Hill, P. (1993). *Newcomers in American schools: Meeting the needs of immigrant youth.* Santa Monica, CA: RAND.

Minicucci, C., & Olsen, L. (1992). Programs for secondary limited English proficient students: A California study. Washington, DC: National Clearing for Bilingual Education.

Moll, L., & González, N. (2004). Engaging life: A funds-of-knowledge approach to multicultural education. In J. Banks & C. Banks (Eds.), *Handbook on research on multicultural education* (2nd ed., pp. 699–713). San Francisco: Jossey-Bass.

Ogbu, J. (1991). Minority status and schooling: A comparative study of immigrant and voluntary minorities. New York: Garland.

Olsen, L. (1997). *Made in America: Immigrant students in our public schools.* New York: The New Press.

Orfield, G., Frankenberg, E., & Lee, C. (2002). The resurgence of school segregation. *Educational Leadership, 60*(4), 1–16.

Pérez, B. (Ed.). (2004). *Sociocultural contexts of language and literacy* (2nd ed.). Mahwah, NJ: Lawrence Erlbaum Associates.

Phelan, P., Davidson, A., & Yu, H. C. (1998). *Adolescents' worlds: Negotiating family, peers, and school.* New York: Teachers College Press.

Portes, A., & Macloud, D. (2005). Educational progress of children of immigrants: The roles of class, ethnicity, and school context. In M. Suárez-Orozco, C. Suárez-Orozco, & D. Qin-Hillard (Eds.), *The new immigration: An interdisciplinary reader* (pp. 309–329). New York: Routledge.

Ruíz-de-Velasco, J., & Fix, M. (2000). *Overlooked and underschooled: Immigrant students in the U.S. secondary schools.* Washington, DC: Urban Institute.

Short, D. (1998). Secondary newcomer programs: Helping recent immigrants prepare for school success. *Digest, EDO-FL-98-06,* 1–5.

Suárez-Orozco, M. (2005). Everything you wanted to know about assimilation but were afraid to ask. In M. Suárez-Orozco, C. Suárez-Orozco, & D. Qin-Hillard (Eds.), *The new immigration: An interdisciplinary reader* (pp. 67–83). New York: Routledge.

Walqui, A. (2000). *Access and engagement: Program design and instructional approaches for immigrant students in secondary schools.* McHenry, IL: Delta Systems.

II

Academic Content Learning

4

Learning English in an English Class

Anne Vega/Merrill

ALEX'S CLASSROOM

Alex grabbed his writing notebook and swung his locker door shut. Fifth hour. Finally. He had been waiting all day for this class. Fifth hour was his sophomore English class. It was the one class he really enjoyed, the only class that really mattered to him. His teacher, Mrs. MacPherson, was pretty cool. She really involved Alex and the other English learners, and she took the time to listen to them whenever they said something in class. Alex never felt dumb in English class. In that class, they wrote about things they cared about and read about things that mattered. After spending all day in classrooms where he felt he was invisible, going to English class was like coming home.

Alex got to class early and helped move back the tables and put the chairs in a circle. The day before the class decided that they were ready for another read around (Christensen, 2000). English class was like that. They got to make choices about what they did in class. They did writing workshop or reading workshop every day, but they got to make decisions about what they wrote and what they read and when they would do wholeclass functions. So far, Alex had written a five-page memoir about moving to America from his home country of Laos, a fiction story about a 15-year-old boy who had joined a gang, a research report on the increase of graffiti in the city, and some poetry. Lately he was writing a lot of poetry. He had also participated in three different literature circles, reading books with his friends and then talking about them. Mrs. MacPherson had really shown him how to "make connections" between what they were reading and what they were writing. That's what she called it: "making connections" or "intertextuality." They were all getting pretty good at it.

It was kind of weird. Mrs. MacPherson was so into the class. She got so excited about what they wrote and what they said in literature circles. At first, everyone kind of rolled their eyes and sometimes after class in the hallways they would mimic her and laugh. "Wow, Alex, what an insight! I never thought about that before!" they would say. Or they would hand each other books and say, "I'm just sure you'll love this book. Why don't you give it a try?" One day they were doing just that, and really loud, when Mrs. MacPherson walked by. She must have heard them and Alex felt really bad about it. He tried to warn the other kids that she was just behind them, but they didn't get it, and they didn't shut up. Mrs. MacPherson just walked on by. When she got just passed them, she turned around, looked right at Alex, and winked. Winked! Then she just kept on walking.

That day in class, she handed Alex a book. "I'm just sure you'll love this book. Why don't you give it a try?" she said. Alex looked at her and she just looked back at him and smiled. Then she said, "Check out Arturo's story. He reminds me of you." Alex looked at the book. It was *An Island Like You* by Judith Ortiz Cofer. Of course he had to read it then. Arturo was a mixed up guy, but he was smart, and in the end he came around. Alex was pretty sure it was a compliment. A few days later he told Mrs. MacPherson he had finished the book—it was that good. "And what did you think of Arturo?" she asked.

"I'm not anything like him. I don't have purple hair," Alex said. She just looked at Alex thoughtfully for a moment. He decided to give her a break. "Okay, I am like him. Just . . . I don't have purple hair." She gave him a great big smile.

"I had forgotten about the purple hair. Arturo is a writer," she said. "Like you." Then she turned around and walked away.

Alex thought about it for a long time. He had never thought of himself as a writer before. He hated to admit it, but he liked the sound of it.

After a while, no one even pretended to try to be cool. Alex thought it was like learning to dance. At first it's hard to dance and look cool. After a while, you just dance. Soon enough, everyone just got into their reading and their writing and didn't worry about how they looked or sounded. You're not a geek if what you're learning about matters. When everyone in the class started seeing themselves reflected in the words that they wrote and read, they didn't have to put up a front anymore. They even got over the fact that Mrs. MacPherson sometimes read them children's books. Some of those books were really well written, and they were about some serious stuff.

Alex recalled not long ago a literature circle group had decided to research the idea of beauty in different cultures. They had read "Beauty Secrets" by Judith Ortiz Cofer (1995) and had gotten into a big discussion about different cultures and what was thought of as beautiful in each. Mrs. MacPherson encouraged the group to do some research, and they ended up doing a big project that they presented to the class. They called it, "The Hegemony of Beauty" and talked about the media and the role it played in saying who was beautiful and who wasn't. The group presentation was really great. Alex learned a lot about the influence of media on what people think and about the values in different cultures.

No one cared about how good your English was, either. It didn't matter. If someone had something to say, he said it however he could. Everyone was patient and listened until they understood. The same with writing. Mrs. MacPherson worked with everyone on their final drafts so that they would be in what she called "standard English." But the way she did it she didn't make you feel bad about it. Alex remembered how she had helped him learn simple past tense. It was during independent writing time. She pulled out Alex's list of skills he was working on and a draft of his writing. She told him she had spoken with a native speaker of Laotian and learned some things about what she called the "language structure." She said that in Laotian, they used "adverbs of time," but not word endings to express time. She asked him if she was right about that. When he thought about it, he realized it was true. They said something like, "Yesterday I run three mile" instead of changing the verb. Alex also realized in Laotian they don't change the plural words, like adding an "s" to "mile". So then Mrs. MacPherson made a page with columns. On the left, she wrote "Laotian" and on the right "standard English"(Christensen, 2003). Then together they wrote examples for past tense and plurals. She told him a little about forming past tense words in English, and then she gave him a list of irregular verbs and showed him where he could find more explanations about simple past tense in the reference books she kept on the book shelf. She told him to think about using proper past tense words in his revisions. Alex had continued to add examples of language structure to the table. Mrs. MacPherson always said to them, "Remember, use what you know to figure out what you don't know." Alex knew Laotian, and it helped him figure things out in English.

Alex had learned a lot of English that way. He was more aware of language structures all the time, even in his reading, when he "read like a writer" (Ray, 2002) as Mrs. MacPherson called it. But he also "read like an English learner" because he looked at not only writing craft, but also language structure. And he loved it that Mrs. MacPherson took the time to learn about his language to help him learn English. His English was really improving. It wasn't just Alex and the other English learners in class that Mrs. MacPherson worked with in this way. It was all of the kids. They all worked on different things in their individual writing conferences, depending on what they needed to learn, and sometimes they worked in small groups on skills. The groups were never just English learners, never the "high" group and the "low" group. It seemed even the kids who spoke English as a mother tongue had things to learn about language.

Alex took a seat in the circle and turned his writing notebook to the page with his poem. He was looking forward to sharing the poem. He wanted to know what the others would think of it. He wasn't nervous about reading his writing in front of his classmates anymore. Mrs. MacPherson was really strict about how they responded. She wouldn't allow them to make fun of each other's writing. It took some time, but now they were starting to respond to each other's writing like they responded to other things that they read. Alex thought some of what they were writing was every bit as good as the books and stories that they read. Mrs. MacPherson thought so, too.

The other kids came to class one by one or in pairs, put their backpacks or books on the tables, and sat in the circle. Mrs. MacPherson joined them. They started class before the bell even rang. It was Anna's turn to take attendance. A student always took attendance so that they could get class started as soon as possible. The class period was never long enough.

Mrs. MacPherson barely waited for the bell to stop ringing when she said, "Okay, let's get started. As always, we'll go around the circle. If you have nothing to read or share today, just say 'pass' and we'll move right along. Let's stay focused so we can get to everyone who wants to read. Remember, when you respond, to focus on the positive. When you write your compliment, please sign your name. Respond to the writer's craft, word choice, or a personal memory or experience it reminded you of. If you're saying your compliment, be sure to address the author, not me. Let's get started. Who wants to go first?" Alex raised his hand quickly. He had been waiting all day to read his poem. He didn't want to wait any longer. Mrs. MacPherson looked at Alex, "Go ahead, Alex. We'll start with you, and then we'll work our way around the circle clockwise."

The room was quiet. Suddenly Alex felt nervous. He liked this poem, and he wanted the class to like it, too. He read,

> "The table is set,
> plates round and empty.
> Waiting.
> The roasted chicken
> is getting cold.
> She shivers,
> watching out the window,
> for the return
> of her Prodigal son."

There was a silence after he read. Some people immediately began writing their compliments on paper. Alex still hadn't got used to the silence after he read, even though he knew the other students were gathering their thoughts. Finally, Maribel spoke.

"What does 'prodigal' mean?"

"It's from the Bible. The bad son finally comes home," Alex replied.

"Oh," Maribel said, "I get it. It's a . . . what's it called?" she looked at Mrs. MacPherson.

"An allusion," she answered.

"Yeah! It's an allusion to the Bible story," Maribel said. She smiled at Alex. "Cool!"

There was another short silence, and then Tae-yul interjected, "So much depends on roasted chicken!" and everyone laughed, including Alex.

Mrs. MacPherson smiled, but then she said, "Tae-yul, say a little more about that. You're on to something there."

Tae-yul couldn't resist rolling his eyes, but then he said, "You know, it's like that book that you read in read aloud, *Love That Dog* (Creech, 2001) . . . "

Anna interrupted him, "No, it's the poem. The Williams poem, 'The Red Wheelbarrow . . . '" (Williams, 1938)

Tae-yul countered, "It's both. Like the kid in *Love That Dog*, so much depended on the dog. Well, in your poem it's like so much depends on the roasted chicken. Like it's all expecting the son, like the chicken is the mother, and her waiting, and her worry. And it's all waiting on the son. So much depends on the chicken, on that dinner, on the son coming home to eat with the family."

Alex smiled at Tae-yul. He got it.

"Nice inter-text-uality, Tae-yul!" Maribel said.

Tae-yul took a breath to respond, but Mrs. MacPherson beat her to it.

"Exactly, Maribel," she said. Tae-yul let his breath out.

Luis spoke up. "It reminds me of the drama moms in *An Island Like You*. A bunch of the stories have these drama moms who are all dramatic when the kid is two minutes past curfew or something."

"Like my mom, geez . . . " said Anna.

"Mine, too!" said Kevin.

"Mine thinks I've been kidnapped if I'm home late!" said Jessica.

"Alex, I like the words 'plates round and empty/the roasted chicken is getting cold' and then 'she shivers'." To me, those are the words that portray a sense of waiting and expectation. Usually if the food is on the table and the table is set, people are already sitting there. The symbolism resides in that missing element."

"Mrs. MacPherson is all like, 'class, class, let's get back to business'!" remarked Patricia.

"Not at all. Alex's poem seems to have struck a chord with many of you. That's wonderful and I'm enjoying your responses. But then I wondered what about the poem, what about the craft, is eliciting this kind of response. So I looked at it again, and I think those words are part of it."

"Oh, so you're studying the craft," said Tae-yul teasingly.

Mrs. MacPherson smiled and said, "Exactly." Then she looked around the circle. "Any more responses to Alex's poem?"

"Yes, Alex. I think you should try a . . . what's it called? Oh yeah, a genre switch. I love the poem, but it really makes me want to hear more. Why is the chicken getting cold? Where is the son and why isn't he home if he knows his whole family is waiting for him?" Anna suggested.

Several students voiced their agreement and looked at Alex.

"I don't know. I hadn't thought about it before. Maybe I'll give it a shot."

"Great idea, Anna. We'll look forward to hearing about the process, Alex. Let's pass our written compliments around to Alex. Nice job, everyone. Now, Sergei?"

Alex gathered his compliments and put them in a neat stack. He couldn't wait to read them. He was pleased with everyone's response. He hadn't thought about doing a genre switch on it, but he liked the idea. In fact, he couldn't wait until the next writing workshop time to give it a try. For now, he was happy to listen to Sergei's new piece. Sergei, Alex knew, would read it in its original Russian first, then paraphrase it. Sergei was a very funny writer, and Alex sat back to listen and enjoy.

COMMITMENTS IN PRACTICE IN ALEX'S CLASSROOM

Secondary teachers work under difficult conditions (Ancess, 2003). With sometimes well over 150 students to teach each day, and very little time in each class period, secondary teachers have to cover a lot of content in a short amount of time. Throw English learners in the mix, and secondary teachers have a tall order to fill. The good news is that it is doable. What it takes is a little change. A little restructuring, a little reconceptualization of time and space in the classroom, and secondary teachers can create vibrant learning communities.

Much can be learned about how to teach English learners from Alex's classroom. In general, several attributes of his classroom make it a viable community of practice. Below we show how these attributes reflect each of our commitments in practice. In the following content chapters we do not discuss each commitment in practice in turn as we do here. We have chosen to spell things out more explicitly in this first content chapter. As a result, this chapter runs longer than subsequent chapters. We hope that the extra scaffolding in this chapter will help guide the reader in seeing classroom implications of our commitments in practice. Moreover, we feel that giving each content chapter a unique structure allows an informative presentation that is not unnecessarily repetitive.

ACTIVE PARTICIPATION

Certain elements enable a community of practice to foster full participation of its members. These include choice, voice, responsibility, and contribution. As each member of a community of practice engages in the academic language, content, and activities in the classroom, each also contributes to the community itself. Below we break down each of these elements in Alex's classroom, showing how the classroom setup fostered active participation of its members.

Choice

Choice is an important element in any learning environment (Fletcher & Portalupi, 2001; Graves, 1990). When students have choice in the classroom, they are likely to have an enhanced sense of ownership over their own learning. That is the ultimate goal of educators: to foster life-long learners. In Alex's classroom, students had choices about what to read and write about. They chose which books and authors to read and how to respond to what they read. They chose genre, topic, and language in what they were writing. They chose which literature circle groups to engage in and when to have wholeclass activities, such as the read around. These kinds of choices are paramount to active participation because they allow students to activate schema and ignite interest for what they are learning. In addition, choice allows students to read and write texts that are relevant to them socially as well as academically. Choice in the language arts classroom is key to successfully supporting English learners.

Voice

Voice is also important in academic learning communities. This holds true in various areas of a classroom community of practice. For example, all members must have a contributing voice in decision making about classroom functions, curriculum decisions, and community activities. Issues of management are resolved through student decision making. Voice helps to foster active participation of all students. In Alex's classroom students came in and sat down quickly and prepared to work. This wasn't because Mrs. MacPherson had a heavy-handed discipline structure. Although Mrs. MacPherson certainly had management structures in place (discussed below), the students' preparedness was also largely because the students were engaged in the processes and anxious to have a chance to participate. They had responsibility, but they also had a voice in classroom decision making. Students had *chosen* to do the read around activity the previous day. In a community of practice, members make suggestions and decisions as a class. Though teachers are the leaders in the community, they often defer decisions to the class as a whole. In this way they are able to give voice and responsibility over to their students. It is Mrs. MacPherson's passion and her caring about her students and their connections to reading and writing that serve her the most when it comes to classroom management. There are a few exceptions. Once the class has made a decision, it is her job to enforce it. She gets class started right away so that the students can have a complete hour of read around—the activity they chose to do. She also is firm about aspects of the community that could be a detriment to its members. For example, she does not allow teasing when students are sharing. As the leader, it is her job to keep her eye on the health of the community. She knows teasing will destroy a risk-free atmosphere, and so does not allow it. Although Mrs. MacPherson gives over much of the decision making to the democratic voice of the classroom, she is also the leader in charge of the community, and her decisions must be based on the balancing act between allowing the students autonomy, responsibility, and choice and keeping the community functioning smoothly. Mrs. MacPherson is aware of this and spends time reflecting on that balance.

Responsibility

The reality of the 50-minute class period makes it paramount that students take over some of the responsibility of their academic communities. All members must have responsibility toward the community, and all members must be able to contribute academically to the community. In Alex's classroom, students got to class early so that they could set up chairs. One student was in charge of attendance. Students had the responsibility to support each others' writing through the read around by writing compliments and discussing their responses to classmates' writing out loud. Classroom communities of practice have a spirit of interdependence, and classmates have the responsibility to help the community run smoothly, as well as to support their own and each others' academic learning and active participation in the community.

Contribution

Active participation in academic communities of practice is fostered as well by contribution. Each student must be able to contribute in her or his own unique way to the community. Alex contributed his poem to the class. In his poem, he made all sorts of connections to other class texts. Community members benefited from this contribution. For Mrs. MacPherson to foster the inclusion of all members, she must know her students and discover ways that each student can contribute. Sergei contributes to the humor in Alex's class, though he chooses to write much of his work in his native Russian. His paraphrasing is funny to the students, and chances are that they will encourage Sergei to write some in English so that they can enjoy his humor even more, reveling in his word choice and how he frames his ideas. As Sergei contributes to his community, he is encouraged to contribute even more (which, in turn, contributes to his acquisition of English and writing skills). In the read around, all students were invited to respond. Students who felt shy about speaking out wrote their responses to Alex.

A beginning student might write, "I like your poem" to Alex. Over time, and through active participation, that student will be able to write more. Mrs. MacPherson's job is to scaffold interactions around reading and writing such that she has an eye for every student's contribution. She finds ways that students can contribute and ways that the community can benefit from each student's strengths. For Sergei, it is his humor in writing. For another student, it may be organization skills, and for another, illustrations. Regardless of English language ability, every student has something to contribute to the community, and every student must be given the opportunity to participate. As this participation is supported, it will also increase.

When choice, voice, responsibility, and contribution are present and accessible to students in classroom communities, as it was in Alex's classroom, active participation is easily fostered in all students.

SOCIAL INTEGRATION

To draw from the multiple strengths and ability levels in a class community, teachers must socially integrate their students. In Alex's classroom, students were grouped heterogeneously in literature circles (which were self-selected), as well as in whole group share (in which students could choose to respond orally or in written form). As we discuss the workshop model below, you will see that there are many ways for the language arts teacher to socially integrate students: through guided literacy groups, in which multilevel students come together on a temporary basis to focus on specific literacy skills and/or strategies; through peer-response groups; and through shared readings and other whole group activities. The workshop model is ideal for social integration of students.

One of the most important tasks of teachers in socially integrated classrooms is to manifest a risk-free environment. In Alex's classroom we saw this through Mrs. MacPherson's firmness that there be no teasing in the class. We also saw how she deferred to the students and their responses to Alex's poem and nudged them to make stronger connections to writing craft through demonstration. A risk-free classroom environment is fostered when the teacher focuses on process over product. When students are given the opportunity to take risks and fail, they are also given the possibility to succeed. Learning activities should not be high stakes. Assessments—and by default, grades—should be based on growth over time and not on high-stakes final products (see Chapter 8 for more on assessment). When students can focus on reading and writing about what they care about within a community they belong to without fear of failure or criticism, they will learn.

INTEGRATED LANGUAGE LEARNING

Students deserve rigor in learning. As English learners actively participate in socially integrated classrooms, the teacher must also encourage rigor in the learning of both content and content-related language. In Alex's classroom, students were given the proper terminology they would need to interact in other communities of practice beyond the classroom. They were also given some of the language of learning. Mrs. MacPherson encouraged them to use the language in their classroom interactions. Alex speaks of "making connections," "intertextuality," and comparing "language structures." Various communities of practice utilize specific discourses. Within classroom communities of practice, students are immersed in the language of the specific discourse in which they are operating. They are encouraged to try the language out, allowed to stumble, and celebrated when they begin to use the language as they interact more fully within the community. Language is access, and teachers must equip students with the discourses of various communities of practice so that they might be given fuller access to outside communities after they leave high school.

In addition, in Alex's classroom there were high teacher expectations that students would engage and connect to various literacy activities. Students actively read, wrote, and talked through various literacy activities. These activities were not (nor should they be) "dumbed down" for English learners who are every bit as capable to interpret, make inferences, and evaluate high-level academic content.

The various expectations, activities, and kinds of talk around content are what give students access to rigor in academic learning. Access is a key concept in learning. As students gain access to the discourse of a learning community, they gain access to the community itself. By the same token, as students gain access to the community, they gain access to learning. The more students are able to interact within a classroom community, the more academic content they will learn, and the more academic language and content they learn, the more access they will have to communities beyond the classroom. It is vital that all students have access to rigor in academic language and content. English learners deserve rigorous classrooms, not remedial classrooms.

SOCIOCULTURAL IDENTITY SUPPORT

As teachers work within the confines of state, national, and district standards (all with a voice in the classroom, to be sure), they must remember to "keep it real." The curriculum in classroom communities of practice should reflect community members. Because the content specific to language arts standards usually revolves around conventions of reading, writing, listening, and speaking, it is usually not difficult to create a curriculum that reflects the students in the classroom. Students can read what they're interested in and write about what's important to them. Inquiry can stem from student interest, and standards can still be met. Classroom teachers must draw from their students' interests and abilities as they navigate new content together. Curriculum is created by the students and is carried out within communities of practice. Curriculum, academic content, and community members interact in a cyclical and reciprocal interplay that is ongoing and increasingly productive. As students learn and grow in areas of interest, so do their literacy skills.

Along with creating a curriculum that reflects each student's unique sense of identity, the language arts teacher must facilitate a sense of affiliation with larger communities of practice in reading and writing. In other words, students must begin to see *themselves* as readers and writers both within the classroom community and within imagined communities of practice within larger contexts. Students interact within new registers, as Alex did, as they learn how to discuss books as real readers do and how to use the writing process as real writers do. Thus, students begin to take on the identity of readers and writers as they interact within the language arts classroom. The more students gain a sense of identity as literate individuals, the more they also identify with wider communities of practice in reading and writing.

In Alex's classroom, there were multiple texts to choose from that represented cherished authors from around the world. Alex's poem was inspired not only by life experiences, but also by a poem by William Carlos Williams. Some students read *An Island Like You* by Judith Ortiz Cofer (1995), a book that highlights the immigrant experiences of several Puerto Rican high school students. When students read books of their choosing (and it's hoped that classroom libraries will support quality multicultural literature) and write pieces from their own experiences, they are allowed to grow not only in language and content knowledge, but also in their own sense of identity as they take on new affiliations.

Classroom teachers must be aware of the tendency in schools to privilege White, middle class curriculum, discourses, and culture in the classroom. When teachers shift to a more inclusive model, all students benefit.

CONNECTIONS TO WIDER CONTEXTS

As students learn and grow in different academic communities of practice, they must also begin to center themselves in wider contexts. As they do so, they come to realize that there are issues of social justice that they can question and change through action. In Alex's classroom, students in a literature circle began to use the text that they shared, and the texts of their own lives to question different cultural norms surrounding beauty. By engaging in such inquiry, they were able to see how their own self-images were manufactured in the hegemony of beauty perpetuated through different means. This kind of inquiry can lead to students taking action such as boycotting magazines, stores, and Web sites that perpetuate the notion of one form of physical beauty. At the same time, students are learning from one another what the notion of "beauty" means in the different cultures represented in the classroom; they are learning about how the definition of "beauty" has changed historically; and they are learning what role the media plays in determining such shared understandings.

As with this inquiry project in Alex's classroom, making connections to wider contexts often happens in the course of students' decision making about their own learning. Classroom teachers need to keep their eye on ways in which students can make such connections to wider contexts.

Following is a table that shows how literacy practices support commitments in practice in general, and more specifically in what we saw in Alex's class.

FEATURES OF LITERACY WORKSHOPS

To honor her commitments in practice, Mrs. MacPherson chose a workshop model for her literacy classes (for additional information, see Atwell, 1998; Five & Egawa, 1998; Fletcher & Portalupi, 2001). The workshop model enabled her to conduct whole group instruction while individualizing instruction for varying abilities in English and academic language through individual conferences and guided reading and writing groups. During reading and writing workshop,

Table 4.1
Literacy Practices—General and in Alex's Class

Commitment	General Practices	Alex's Class
Active participation	Student choice, voice, responsibility, and contribution; small group work; individual projects; process learning	All students read; all students write; all students engage in multiple literacy activities individually and in small and whole class groupings
Social integration	Small group work; think-pair-share; silent dialogue; scaffolded participation; heterogeneous groupings	Literature circles; small group inquiry; whole group share (read around); guided reading; guided writing
Integrated language learning	Scaffolded whole group discussions; word study (vocab); word walls; shared reading/writing; grammar for craft; writing craft	Language included in class activities (making connections, genre switch, intertextuality); individual conferences; guided reading and writing groups; shared reading and writing
Sociocultural identity support	Multicultural literature; inclusion of student strengths and interests in curriculum	Choice in writing activities; choice in literature; multicultural classroom library; personal response to literature
Connections to wider contexts	Individual inquiry projects; community service projects	Small group inquiry on gender roles and the hegemony of beauty; intertextual connections

Mrs. MacPherson was able to conduct ongoing assessments from which to plan instruction. Perhaps you've heard of the workshop model before and wondered whether it is viable for English learners. A workshop that runs efficiently is very effective for keeping English learners involved in community activities and events. Below we describe attributes and individual literacy activities often found in a workshop model. We go into detail here as the workshop model can be used effectively in virtually any content area.

ORGANIZATIONAL STRUCTURES

For communities of practice to function efficiently, the teacher must initiate organizational structures (Atwell, 1998; Fletcher & Portalupi, 2001). Though organizational structures may be changed by the community as it operates throughout the school year, at the beginning of the year the organizational structure is the responsibility of the teacher. In communities of practice in language arts, students are often engaged in different activities at the same time. One student may be drafting, another editing, another engaged in a peer conference, or several students may be reading silently while a small group is engaged in a literature circle. The only way 30-plus adolescents will be able to function in a workshop-like atmosphere is if there are some well-established organizational structures. There must be a place for supplies, a place for conferencing, a means by which the class can move tables and chairs to accommodate various small and large group functions. There must be structures for record keeping, folders to keep drafts of writing, lots of paper, and highlighters. Computers for conducting research and word processing are a definite plus. Routines must be established with an ongoing process for solving problems as they arise. For example, if literature circles or peer conferencing become too loud so that others can't concentrate on drafting or reading, what viable solutions can the class find?

Once the classroom setup and structures are established, the teacher must coordinate the class schedule in such a way as to ensure generous amounts of time for workshops. The community members must have routines that are predictable enough that they can plan ahead for their projects. Class members can each take on jobs to help facilitate a smoothly running community. The right to time and space to engage in literacy processes with the community is coupled with responsibility toward that community.

Built into these setups must be opportunities for collaboration and peer support. Rules must be established so that every student can utilize class time to further their endeavors in literacy processes and in language acquisition. Organization is an important part of a successful room community of practice in language arts.

Daily Reading and Writing

Though this may seem self-explanatory, the concept of daily opportunities to read and write warrants discussion. Just as with the saying, "success builds success," the same holds true with reading and writing. Reading builds reading, and writing builds writing. The more students are involved in reading, writing, listening, and speaking about books and writings that matter to them, the more they will learn. Reading and writing, and the talk that revolves around them, must happen daily (Graves, 1990). This holds true especially in secondary classrooms in which there is less than an hour a day dedicated to language arts. Since instruction about skills occurs in the context of what students are reading and writing, there need not be large amounts of time set aside for them. However, to accomplish the vast amounts of reading and writing that must occur for language acquisition and the learning of academic content, time must be set aside daily for reading and writing. Some secondary teachers choose to alternate days of reading and writing workshop (Atwell, 1998) so that there is a predictable routine and enough time for both.

Literature Circle

One of the activities that Mrs. MacPherson's class engaged in was literature circles (Peterson & Eeds, 1990; Smith, 1990). Literature circles are a great way for students to interact and build community around books. There are different ways to organize literature circles. The teacher can choose a theme and pick several books for students to choose from, or students can choose books themselves. Language arts teachers who team teach with social studies teachers will often choose historical fiction that matches themes and/or content. In literature circles, students read the book of choice, and then meet in small groups to discuss different literary or textual elements in the book. Literature circles in classrooms are much like book clubs in literary communities of practice outside the classroom. They are a great way to foster active participation as well as to create heterogeneous groupings, two of our commitments in practice. Students who struggle with reading can read with a buddy or listen to the book on tape so that they can engage in more sophisticated discussions about books of interest to them even if they aren't yet able to read them on their own.

Minilessons

In a workshop model most class time is given over to actual literacy practices. Instruction is given in context of specific reading and writing activities. Minilessons are teacher-directed, whole group lessons that focus on specific skills or practices in literacy or on procedures for managing the workshop itself (Hindley, 1996). For example,

Mrs. MacPherson had done a minilesson demonstrating a genre switch for her students. She might also prepare a minilesson on proper use of quotation marks or using context to figure out the meaning of a word. Minilessons consist of instruction the whole class needs. Once a skill, practice, or procedure is demonstrated, the class goes straight into independent reading or writing time where they can gain some guided support. Minilessons are a place for direct instruction, but are purposefully short so that students can go directly into supported reading and writing activities.

Shared Reading/Writing

Shared reading (Holdaway, 1982) is generally thought of as an approach to teach phonics and word study in context for younger children. However, shared reading and writing are excellent strategies for secondary students as well. In shared reading, the teacher brings in a text, say a poem or a song, and the class reads the text together. The text can then be used for word study, interpretation, or discussion of literary elements. Choral readings can be especially effective in teaching English learners syntactic structures in English. Shared readings also can be great community building activities.

Shared writing works in much the same way. Teachers can engage the students in some aspect of the writing process through modeling as they write on the board or overhead projector, including students in writing decisions as they go. Shared reading and writing are great ways to focus on word study and the integration of language and content.

Guided Reading/Writing

One of the greatest tools of the workshop teacher is guided reading/writing groups. These groups are heterogeneous, temporary groups that the teacher assembles to work on specific skills in reading and writing. For example, students in Mrs. MacPherson's class who want to learn more about genre switch might get together in a small group for instruction. The groups can work on meaning-making strategies for reading, spelling strategies, or the elements of persuasive or expository writing. Guided reading and writing groups are an excellent way for teachers to individualize instruction according to need. English learners benefit from the extra scaffolding as well as from the heterogeneous groupings.

Independent Reading/Writing

All students need time to read and write. During independent reading and writing time, the teacher conducts guided groups and individual conferences while the rest of the group reads or writes independently, working on various projects. Teachers need to have a viable classroom library full of literature of diverse genres and representing different cultures. Mrs. MacPherson included multicultural children's literature in her classroom library and in her read aloud and literature circle. Children's literature is beneficial for writing classrooms studying craft in writing, even in the secondary classroom. Having an accessible classroom library is very important for a viable workshop. Independent reading and writing time allows the teacher to individualize and guide instruction of literacy in context.

Individual Conferences

Individual conferences are extremely important to a well-run workshop. Teachers conference individually with several students each class period, keeping notes of the conference while they coach students as they practice individual skills. For example, Mrs. MacPherson found early in the year that although Alex could decode text quite well, his comprehension skills in reading were quite low. She conducted a miscue analysis (Goodman & Goodman, 1994; Weaver, 2002) and discovered that Alex was overrelying on his graphophonic cueing system. In individual reading conferences, Mrs. MacPherson was able to teach Alex more meaning-making strategies. His comprehension skills had developed rapidly. In continuing individual conferences Mrs. MacPherson monitored Alex's progress. In his most recent reading conference she read with Alex from his history textbook and they talked about the kinds of discourse found in textbooks and how to make meaning from this different kind of text. The conference had gone so well that Mrs. MacPherson was planning a guided reading group for a small group of students who were struggling in their other content area classes. The guided reading group would learn about meaning-making strategies for textbooks that they found difficult to navigate.

Individual conferences are also important for assessment purposes. Files can be kept on each student as they learn new skills so that the teacher knows what the students are doing well and what they need to continue to work on. Such files have proved indispensable for teachers in districts that monitor standards closely: They are proof that the content that required is being taught. Alex had worked on verb tense in his writing, and Mrs. MacPherson monitored his writing drafts to see how well he was progressing on this skill. She was able to provide evidence of Alex's progress over time and could discern what he still needed to work on. She generated instruction from the needs she saw in her students' reading and writing as she jotted down notes from conferences, guided groups, and whole group discussions. Individual conferences help teachers individualize instruction in classrooms that by their very nature represent great diversity in ability levels and literacy experiences.

In all, literacy workshops are an excellent framework for living the commitments in practice and meeting the needs of the community of practice and each individual within the community.

A WORD ABOUT CLASSROOM MANAGEMENT

In our visits to classrooms over the years, we have observed and learned from excellent teachers. Now and again, however, we find that classroom practice that is well situated in terms of research often undermines its own effectiveness through management styles that are overly authoritarian or too loose. We have found that both situations serve to undermine the community because both extremes create a high-risk environment for students, especially for English learners. Below, we discuss attributes of classroom management that are most conducive to meeting the needs of all students in the classroom.

A Democratic Classroom

For our communities of practice to run effectively, it is important that there be a balance of rights (Faltis, 2006) among members. That means that no one in the classroom becomes an authoritarian leader, usurping the rights of fellow members. Matters of discipline must be handled in a democratic fashion. Rules are devised by and for the community and deviations from those rules must be handled by the community. The teacher's job, then, is to create a forum for dealing with issues that are affecting the community's ability to run smoothly. Class meetings can be used for dealing with issues that are disruptive to the community. The community must then problem solve in a manner in which no member is degraded, and the community itself can function.

Students must often be taught interpersonal skills and methods for solving problems with one another. Although democratic problem solving takes time, it is vital for students who will become participating members of our local, state, and national communities. In addition, problem-solving strategies help strengthen our academic communities of practice. A smoothly functioning community of practice is a classroom in which students are learning effectively. In short, democratic discipline is not a waste of time.

THE TEACHER'S ROLE

Though each member of the community has rights and responsibilities, teachers assume an extremely important role. They must fully know each student and be able to draw from what they know to help students make connections to the content. In Alex's case, Mrs. MacPherson had a clear understanding of what skills Alex needed to work on. She catered her instruction to Alex, learning more about his native language in order to support his learning. She knew he needed work on past tense, and she taught him past tense functions in English by relying on his schema about his native language and by teaching him past tense within the context of his own writing. She also gave him the metalanguage he needed to have control over his own learning. Further, Mrs. MacPherson knew enough about Alex's personal life to hand him a book with a character in it who might become a metaphor for Alex in his decision-making processes in his own life. To do that, Mrs. MacPherson also had to have a wide repertoire of books to draw from.

Mrs. MacPherson taught the whole class through demonstration in their read around. She modeled tying the effect of the writing craft to the actual written word in Alex's poem, reminding the students that within reader–text transactions, the text plays an important role.

At this point, Mrs. MacPherson will need to keep track of Alex's progress in his evolving writing, from skills (such as grammar and spelling) to craft (the power in his writing). To do this, she will need to keep detailed records of her conferences with Alex and her ongoing assessments of his progress. She will also need to keep records of his evolving reading, taking note of his input in class discussions, literature circles, and the connections he's making from reading to his own writing. These ongoing assessments will be the basis for her instruction with both Alex and the larger community.

In a community of practice, the teacher's role is immense, and it is paramount to students' growth as readers, writers, listeners, and speakers, as well as citizens of the world.

The Literature Connection

Just as literature plays a vital role in our communities of practice beyond the classroom, literature plays a leading role in our language arts classrooms (Peterson & Eeds, 1990). Alex's class had a number of books and poems to draw from in their discussions. They had experienced these pieces not only as read alouds (yes, read alouds belong in high school, as well) and shared readings, but also within their literature circles. For a community of practice to flourish, literature must be present, cherished, and studied by the community. Touchstone pieces give the class points of reference for their discussions. These pieces help guide the community as a whole in their understandings and interpretation of literature as well as in their own writing.

One of the most important jobs of teachers is to be readers and writers themselves. When teachers are actively engaged in the reading and writing processes, they are able to engage with their classroom community more fully. They can slip out of their role of teacher and experience the reading and writing processes as a reader and writer. They will be able to contribute to the community on a different level, and they will also benefit from the community's support of their own processes.

Teachers need to know what literature will appeal to their students. Various books and poems can be recommended to students as they grow and evolve in their own reading and writing. The following book list will help move the high school library toward a more diverse representation of literature. These books are great for literature circles or independent reading.

A LOOK AT STUDENTS NEW TO ENGLISH

We believe that isolating beginners for skill and drill practice is detrimental to their learning of language and content. By the same token, immersing beginners to the English language in classrooms that don't take the time to scaffold language and content learning is often isolating. Students are left behind when they don't understand what's going on around them. On the other hand, we have been witness to beginners

MOVING BEYOND THE TRADITIONAL

Traditional high school reading lists often lack diversity. Diversifying reading lists will help prepare students more effectively for college-level reading. Try adding some of these books and authors to your college prep reading lists.

Alvarez, Julia *In the Time of the Butterflies; How the Garcia Girls Lost Their Accents*

Anaya, Rudolfo *Bless Me, Ultima*

Bagdasarian, Adam *Forgotten Fire*

Buck, Pearl S. *The Good Earth*

Cisneros, Sandra *The House on Mango Street; Caramelo*

Cofer, Judith Ortiz, *An Island Like You; The Latin Deli*

Curtis, Christopher Paul *The Watsons Go to Birmingham; Bud, Not Buddy*

Dumas, Firoozeh *Funny in Farsi*

Jiménez, Francisco *The Circuit*; *Breaking Through*

Ho, Minfong *The Clay Marble*

Hurston, Zora Neale *Their Eyes Were Watching God*

Lowry, Lois *Number the Stars*

Morrison, Toni *Beloved; The Bluest Eye*

Na, An *A Step from Heaven*

Nye, Naomi Shihab *Habibi*

Park, Linda Sue *A Single Shard; When My Name Was Keoko*

Ryan, Pam Munoz *Esperanza Rising; Becoming Naomi Leon*

Soto, Gary *Baseball in April and Other Stories; Taking Sides; Pacific Crossing*

Staples, Suzanne Fisher *Shabanu: Daughter of the Wind*

Tan, Amy *The Joy Luck Club; Saving Fish from Drowning*

Walker, Alice *The Color Purple*

Williams-Garcia, Rita *Like Sisters on the Home Front*

growing by leaps and bounds when they are immersed in a community that provides scaffolding along with opportunities for contribution to the community.

One of the most expedient ways of bringing beginners into a community of practice in language arts is through their native language. Even beginners who are the only speaker of their native language can be offered the opportunity to express themselves in their native language as they increasingly become contributing members of the community (a more detailed discussion of native language in the language arts classroom follows). In the meantime, they can be given jobs that aren't bound by language and opportunities to talk and communicate with classmates in interactions that are tied to concrete experiences.

Classroom communities of practice are an ideal place for beginners to make approximations. If students want to write about their immigration story, for example, they can write it in very simple language:

> *When I came to America I was very nervous. The high school was very big. I spoke no English. All I heard is English. I missed my home. I missed my friends. I was very homesick. Now I have made some friends and I feel better. But I still miss my home.*

Students writing even these very simple stories can participate in the writing process, publication, and sharing of their stories. Over time, their stories will become increasingly complex, and their English will grow as they participate in their community literacy activities. Teachers of beginning English learners who build a community around writing are often surprised at how quickly their beginners are able to produce longer pieces of writing in English. During workshop, the teacher works with small groups or one-on-one with students to work on skills within the context of their own emerging language. Through use of native language and approximations in English, beginners are able to participate fully in the community of practice from the start.

TEACHING STUDENTS WITH NONPARALLEL SCHOOLING EXPERIENCES

As the number of immigrants increases, so does the diversity of school experiences that they bring with them. Teachers are increasingly faced with students who have little to no schooling experiences (see Tables 3.1 and 3.2). These students have a tall order to fill: huge gaps in academic discourses and little knowledge of how to "play" school. Nonparallel students benefit from predictable structures and routines. Literacy classrooms that rely on a workshop model are ideal for underschooled students because the structure of workshops is very predictable. Students come to know what to expect on any given day, and because of this feel safer taking risks in their reading and writing. In fact, all students benefit from predictable routines.

Nonparallel students are often in great need of literacy skills. The workshop model such as what Mrs. MacPherson had in place gives teachers the chance to work with nonparallel students individually in conferences or in small, guided literacy groups. In addition, relying on multiple texts and genres, including children's literature and books that reflect students' background experiences, gives underschooled students more access to the written word. Nonparallel students bring a diversity of experiences and perspectives to discussions about books, so literature circles, read alouds, and shared readings allow them to add their ideas to discussions such that the whole class community benefits.

Activities that help support nonparallel students gain access to more sophisticated texts are buddy readers, books on tape, adult volunteers who read with them, scribes who write or type for them (such as the language experience approach; see Dixon & Nessel, 1983), and the like. With a little support, students with gaps in their academic knowledge can grow exponentially and become full members of classroom communities.

THE ROLE OF NATIVE LANGUAGE

Members of a community of practice need access to the practice. It is paramount that English learners who are just learning English be invited into the community. One way to facilitate this invitation is the use of native language. Beginning English learners can have access to the community of readers and writers if they are invited to participate any way that they can, be it through native language or through contextualized reading and writing activities.

As with any community of practice, students must gain a sense of identity with the practice. Thus, for English learners to gain a sense of identity as readers and writers, they must participate in a community that reads and writes. Secondary English learners who are literate in their native language can participate as readers and writers in that language. They can write in various genres for various purposes and to various audiences in their native language. They can read books in their native language and participate in literature circles and other literacy activities with English-speaking peers.

Teachers who write with their beginning English learners are often surprised at how much their students can and will write—in English—when they have a choice of what to write about, a risk-free place to rely on the writing process, and a community of people to read and write with. Adolescents want to be included, and as they are included they will contribute significantly to the community of practice. Because our classrooms are increasingly diverse, English is the language all community members have in common. The desire to belong to the community and the automatic, risk-free ability to participate will help facilitate English learning, as well as the learning of academic content that occurs mostly in English. Communities of practice in language arts that have the good fortune of having all members with two common languages can function bilingually, with content and academic learning occurring in both English and the other language.

Summary

In this chapter we've portrayed what our commitments in practice look like in the language arts classroom. It is our hope that we have conveyed a sense of what's possible even in secondary schools that are traditionally structured in terms of time and space. We are convinced that the unique needs of each student can be met and that English learners can become full members of classroom communities of practice in any content area.

There are several key points to remember in creating classroom communities of practice that are inclusive:

- Students need active participation within classroom communities of practice. Content-based talk and activities should be interactive, active, and rigorous.

- To foster full participation within classroom communities students need choice, voice, responsibility, and contribution.

- Social integration among multiple ability levels as well as cultural and linguistic backgrounds will provide increased access to content and academic learning.

- Adolescents should see themselves reflected in the curriculum. Providing choice in reading, writing, and inquiry projects will help students become full members in a classroom community. Academic classroom communities can provide relevance and a sense of affinity and identity to all students.

- We can help students connect to wider contexts through curriculum that engages them in issues of social justice and change through action. Providing a sense of identity to wider contexts will help students gain membership in communities of practice beyond the classroom.

- Workshop models are conducive to fostering membership in classroom communities of practice. In workshop models, individual academic and linguistic needs of English learners can be met within a community of students who read and write for various purposes.

- Democratic classrooms help foster commitments in practice such that teachers do not become overbearing, usurping the rights of community members, nor do they become weak leaders, allowing a chaotic classroom to usurp the rights of community members.

- The language arts community of practice can foster membership of all students, including those new to English or with nonparallel schooling experiences. *Access and inclusion* in academic classroom communities of practice are vital to the academic success of English learners.

- Native language can be used to provide access to community membership and academic content.

English learners can gain access to academic content the moment they first walk through your classroom door. Our challenge to you is to adapt your own practice to foster membership and rigorous learning among all members in your unique classroom community of practice.

Activities

1. Many districts still use the "dead White men" curriculum, relying exclusively on western European classics. Examine the various types of literature in your classroom and school library. How many multicultural books are there? Is there a diversity of authors, cultures, genders, and classes represented? Which ones have you read and which do you recommend using? What can you add to your collection to make it more representative and relevant to English learners in your school?

2. Some programs delay English learners' experiences with authentic literacy until they have mastered the conventions, such as spelling and grammar. In what ways can such a delay be detrimental to English learners? What other options are there?

3. With the onset of high-stakes standardized testing, some districts feel the pressure to focus on skills in isolation. Design a language arts unit that teaches skills and conventions in context. Then, search through district and state guidelines to determine which standards are addressed in the unit.

4. Today's classrooms represent a wide range of experiences and ability levels. How can you organize the classroom so that learners' needs are met in an inclusive, heterogeneous environment?

5. Draw a floor plan of your ideal classroom. Be sure to arrange space for large group, small group, and individualized instruction. How can you arrange the space to support a classroom community of practice in language arts?

6. Brainstorm ways to include native language supports for English learners in the language arts classroom.

References

Ancess, J. (2003). *Beating the odds: High schools as communities of commitment.* New York: Teachers College Press.

Atwell, N. (1998). *In the middle: New understandings about writing, reading, and learning.* Portsmouth, NH: Heinemann.

Christensen, L. (2003). The politics of correction. *Rethinking schools online, 18(6).* http://www.rethinkingschools.org, retrieved on Nov 2, 2004.

Christensen, L. (2000) *Reading, writing, and rising up: Teaching about social justice and the power of the written word.* Milwaukee, WI: Rethinking Schools.

Creech, S. (2001). *Love that dog: A novel.* New York: Scholastic.

Cofer, J. O. (1995). *An island like you: Stories of the barrio.* New York: Puffin Books.

Dixon, C., & Nessel, D. (1983). *Language experience approach to reading (and writing): Language experience reading for second language learners.* Hayward, CA: Alemany Press.

Faltis, C. (2006). *Teaching English language learners in elementary school communities: A join-fostering approach.* Upper Saddle River, NJ: Pearson Merrill Prentice Hall.

Five, C. L., & Egawa, K. (1998). Reading and writing workshop. *School Talk, 3(4).*

Fletcher, R., & Portalupi, J. (2001). *Writing workshop: The essential guide.* Portsmouth, NH: Heinemann.

Graves, D. (1990). *A fresh look at writing.* Portsmouth, NH: Heinemann.

Hindley, J. (1998). *In the company of children.* York, ME: Stenhouse.

Holdaway, D. (1982). Shared book experience: Teaching reading using favorite books. *Theory into practice 21*(4), 293–300.

Goodman, Y. M., & Goodman, K. S. (1994). To err is human: Learning about language processes by analyzing miscues. In R. B. Ruddell, M. R. Ruddell, & H. Singer (Eds.), *Theoretical models and processes of reading* (4th ed., pp. 104–123). Newark, DE: International Reading Association.

Peterson, R., & Eeds, M. (1990). *Grand conversations: Literature groups in action.* New York: Scholastic.

Ray, K. W. (2002). *What you know by heart: How to develop curriculum for your writing workshop.* Portsmouth, NH: Heinemann.

Smith, K (1990). Entertaining a text: A reciprocal process. In K. Short & K. M. Pierce (Eds.), *Talking about books* (pp. 17–25). Portsmouth, NH: Heinemann.

Weaver, C. (2002). *Reading process & practice.* Portsmouth, NH: Heinemann.

Williams, W. C. (1938) The red wheelbarrow. *Collected poems: 1909–1939, Volume 1,* New York: New Directions Publishing Corporations.

5

Teaching and Learning Math for English Learners

Anne Vega/Merrill

MARLENA'S STORY

According to her mother, Marlena had a prodigious memory. At age 14, Marlena could remember details about where she grew up—Cofradia de Sutchlitlán, a small village outside the capitol city of Colima, Colima in Mexico. Marlena's family, which included her mother and father and two younger brothers, moved to Colima when she was five, but she could tell stories about herself and her brothers and the *rancho* they lived on. In the summer of her 13th birthday, Marlena and her family moved again. This time, they packed up their belongings and moved up north, settling in the city where their cousins had gone to several years before. No one in Marlena's family had ever known anyone who had gone beyond the sixth grade in Mexico; there was no need for schooling beyond that when you worked on a farm. Marlena was the first to complete the sixth grade, and the first in her family to continue on to secundaria (middle school), where she studied until the summer she moved up north. Marlena's ability to remember what she learned in school made her one of the top students of her class.

When Marlena's mother signed her up for high school, the community worker recommended that she attend the Newcomer Program to gain an orientation to high school and to learn English. Marlena had never studied English before, but she was eager to learn it. Marlena had goals: She wanted to be an architect, to design and build low-income homes for poor people in Mexico. Learning English was a struggle at first, but once Marlena believed that she had figured out some of the basic rules, she breezed through the various levels of English. Her strength was vocabulary; she could easily memorize 10 words a day, and when new words were presented in readings and discussion, she picked those up as well. After a full year in the Newcomer Program, Marlena was deemed ready for all-English academic classes. Her English still marked her as an English learner, but that didn't get in the way of her determination to finish high school and become an architect.

Every school subject interests Marlena; she is like a sponge when it came to learning something new. In Marlena's geometry class, the culminating topic is Understanding Slope, which she refers to as "eslope." Marlena's geometry teacher this year is Mrs. Diamante, a long-time math teacher who is dedicated to working mainly with English learners. In Mrs. D's class, Marlena is one of 10 students who are still learning English. The remaining 20 students are native English speakers.

To prepare the students for the complexity of using the equation $y = mx + b$ to graph the slope of a line, Mrs. Diamante spent several weeks reviewing and building background knowledge about how to locate integers on a number line, add positive and negative integers, recognize the absolute value of numbers, and use the additive inverse rule. Most of the students are familiar with these concepts, but need more practice to become fully fluent in their uses.

Mrs. D finds that many students also need additional work on writing mathematical definitions, so she has some of the students use their own whiteboards to write out formal definitions of key concepts as the class progresses through activities. She models this on an overhead and helps students to see the difference between personal definitions and formal definitions. Moreover, she constantly refers students to the word wall that they are creating, putting up new vocabulary words along with any symbols associated with them.

Following the work on number lines, Mrs. Diamante moves on to graphs and how they are used to represent data points; namely, how to plot ordered pairs on a coordinate graph. This unit introduces many new concepts that require considerable practice. Mrs. Diamante introduces the idea of graphs by rolling out an 8′×10′ tarp that she has prepared with an x axis (horizontal) and a y axis (vertical) with numbers from zero to +/− 10 on each of the axes. She also has a graph showing on the overhead. After going over the orientation of x and y and tarp behavior rules, she gives the steps for plotting an ordered pair of numbers on the graph.

Marlena volunteers to stand on the ordered pair of (3,2), counting three to the right and two up. Mrs. Diamante plots that point on the overhead graph. These actions are repeated several times so that the class can physically participate in the plotting of a point as well as see Mrs. Diamante indicate the points on her graph. Later on in small groups, students practice plotting points and connecting lines to draw geometric figures.

"How does this go again?" says Miguel, asking about (−4,6) and looking to Marlena for help. "Do we go over first or down first?"

Marlena thinks about how to say it, and then replies, "I always remember that x comes before y in the alphabet. That way, I know where is the first number, and after that, I count to the second number. If is negative the number, I count this way [pointing to numbers left and below zero], and if is positive, I go this way [pointing to the right and above zero]."

"It's the negatives that get me messed up," says Tracy, another group member.

Miguel nods, adding, "Me too, but if I can remember the order, I can do this right."

"Let's write this stuff in our journals," say Marlena. Miguel, Tracy, and Marlena each write out the procedure they use to plot numbers, using precise language and following the model that Mrs. D has instilled in them for working with algorithms: "I discovered that . . . , I noticed that . . . , the strategy I use is . . . "

Mrs. D watches how the students are making progress as they work with graphs and plotting points, paying attention to who needs additional practice and especially to how students are beginning to use the vocabulary (e.g., x and y coordinates, x axis, quadrant, etc.) as they interact in groups and write out their work on their whiteboards. In addition, she reads and responds to the students' journal entries about what they noticed and what they are still figuring out. Once she is satisfied that the students have become thoroughly familiar with plotting numbers and using graphs, she moves on to the next set of activities, which further prepare students for working with equations involved in calculating slope by introducing the concepts of *rise* and *run* in order to plot a line.

To begin, Mrs. D once again brings out the 8′×10′ tarp (to serve as the plane), which is taped with *x* and *y* axes and marked with a point of origin (zero) and positive and negative integers. She also has thick string available for each student. Every student has a whiteboard (12″×18″) to write out formulae and vocabulary; dry erasers are available for all students. By now, the word wall is filled with power vocabulary words related to coordinate geometry, along with simple pictures and corresponding mathematical symbols. Mrs. D has also prepared word cards in different colors to introduce new vocabulary and to review words that students have already seen.

Mrs. Diamante begins by going over appropriate tarp behavior and then has students count off by 3s so that one third have vocabulary cards, one third have whiteboards, and one third are on the tarp. The 1s are on the graph, the 2s are at the perimeter with vocabulary cards, and the 3s are also at the perimeter with whiteboards and their journals. There are two vocabulary cards for each word, and students who have identical word cards are not sitting next to one another.

After reviewing some of the vocabulary by having individual students place a word card on the plane according to its meaning, Mrs. Diamante has one student, beginning at the point of origin, move up one and to the right one. The second student begins at origin, and this time both students move up one, and to the right one. The third student begins at origin, but this time all three move up one and to the right one. However, this time, Mrs. Diamante says "Rise positive one, run positive one."

"What did I do different this time?" asks Mrs. Diamante.

"You said 'rise' and 'run,'" several students respond. This introduction to rise and run causes a great deal of uneasiness, because many students don't grasp the difference between plotting a point and plotting a line. The fourth student begins at origin and all four students now rise positive one, run positive one. There are a few AHA! moments, as the four students begin to form a straight line. She continues having all 10 students rise one, run one. Once this is accomplished, she has the students stretch out a string tautly so that everyone can clearly see the line they have created. To ease the students' anxiety, Mrs. Diamante takes a few minutes to explain how a positive rise over a positive run leads to a positive slope and writes out on her whiteboard, 1/1. While the students stand on the tarp, those with whiteboards write out definitions of *positive slope*, *positive rise*, and *positive run*, and check their work with a partner.

"Why we go up first, before over, when before we going over first, then up?" Felipe asks Marlena, who is sitting next to him on the floor.

"Porque, este, esta vez estamos trazando una línea; antes trazamos un punto" [Because, um, this time we are plotting a line; last time we plotted a point], she answers him in Spanish. "Remember the line," she adds.

"Órale, Marlena" [Cool, Marlena], says Felipe, feeling a bit clearer about what is going on at the tarp.

Mrs. Diamante has the students rotate their positions, so that the students who were doing vocabulary are now on the tarp. This time, she starts by having one student move down one and to the left one. When the third student is ready to move, she says, "Rise negative one, run negative one." Here she asks Tamika, who has a whiteboard describing what she noticed about how rise and run works.

"Rise can be up or down. I think it depends on if it's a negative or positive number. The same with run, it can go right or left," says Tamika.

"Remember, guys, you always rise in the morning before you run to the bathroom," Mrs. Diamante reminds the class jokingly, and she writes on her whiteboard $-1/-1$. After all the students have completed one negative rise, one negative run movement, she asks the students with whiteboards to write out what they understand about rise over run and has the 10 students again stretch out a string to show that a line has been created.

She then turns to Marlena and asks, "Based on what we know about positive slope, what would we call a slope where both the rise and run are negative numbers?"

Haltingly, Marlena says, "Positive eslope?"

"Why do you think it is called positive slope?" Mrs. Diamante probes.

"Is because negative divided into negative is always positive," Marlena says almost as a question.

"Right, Marlena, the line will rise. In other words, when the points on the line are both positive or both negative, the slope of the line is positive. What else can you tell about the slope based on the rise over run, say about the direction of the slope?"

Mrs. Diamante continues the discussion asking about a negative divided by a negative, and comparing positive to negative slope, pointing out positions of each on her whiteboard graph. To check for understanding, she asks students with the vocabulary cards, negative and positive slope, to place their cards on the tarp in the corresponding quadrants. In the meantime, students are talking about the concepts in their small groups, noticing how the direction of the slope depends on the equation of run over rise.

Following this, the students rotate, placing a new group of 10 students on the tarp. Again, Mrs. Diamante starts with one student on the point of origin: "Move up one and to the left one." She instructs the second student to do the same. With the third student, she shifts to "rise positive one, run negative 1." She continues until all students have completed the movement, and they have stretched a string to create a new line, creating a negative slope. Because some students are still confused, she works on her whiteboard to show that dividing a positive number by a negative number always results in a negative answer, resulting in a negative slope.

Mrs. Diamante rotates the groups a final time, with the original group back on the tarp, and the other groups either working on vocabulary or writing on their whiteboards. For this final rotation, the students on the tarp, one by one, rise negative one and run positive one. As they are doing this,

Mrs. Diamante asks the students with whiteboards to write whether they think the slope will be positive or negative and why. In her head, Marlena decides that it will be negative because a negative number divided by a positive number is always negative, meaning the slope is negative too. Many of the students write that it will be a negative slope, but can't give a good reason. And, as Mrs. Diamante knows, the reason is much more complicated than whether or not the answer is positive or negative. But, that understanding won't come until much later, when students begin to understand slope as a rate of change, which involves calculating the equation of a line using $y = mx + b$. Once students reach this level of understanding, they will then begin to apply this knowledge to real life issues, such as designing a handicap ramp for wheelchair access at the local community center and figuring out the most efficient times to make long distance calls with various telephone companies.

A CLOSER LOOK AT MARLENA'S GEOMETRY CLASS

The vignette you just read shows how Marlena and other students were actively engaged in building background knowledge to prepare them for graphing linear equations, determining the midpoint between two points in a coordinate system, and determining rates of change in a graph of a linear function. This is pretty sophisticated math, requiring a deep understanding of spatial relationships on a coordinate plane. What Mrs. Diamante did in these early lessons to engage the English learners in her class helped them not only to participate as mathematicians, but also to acquire English by using the language they were learning for meaningful purposes. Let's examine more carefully what happened in Marlena's class to see how Mrs. Diamante drew on the commitments in practice to invite English learners into real and imagined mathematics communities of practice, to help them see themselves as real readers and writers of English. To be sure, Mrs. Diamante referred to all students as mathematicians, but what is important is how she assisted their identity affiliations with mathematic communities, participating in the kinds of language and computational practices that mathematicians, real and imagined, use to figure out mathematical problems.

What You Didn't See

Before beginning, however, it might be worthwhile to point out what you didn't see in Mrs. Diamante's class. This is not a traditional high school math class in the sense that students are not seated individually in rows with all eyes up front, focusing on the teacher who is transmitting information to them using the whiteboard and overhead. This kind of classroom, which is all too prevalent in many secondary schools, has a teacher space and a student space. The teacher works from his or her space, and students are expected to remain stationary in their designated space (their desks). Talking among students is discouraged, as is sharing of ideas and materials. The teacher has all of the content area knowledge and relies on content area standards and commercial texts to organize teaching and learning activities. Students "practice" what they have been taught using worksheets and end-of-the-chapter exercises. In this kind of math class, the onus on learning concepts, operations, and vocabulary is entirely on the students, not the result of interaction between teacher and the students or among students working as a community of learners. The math teacher is simply that. He or she is not considered to be a language teacher, a reading teacher, a writing teacher, or an English-as-a-second-language teacher.

A More Integrative Approach to Math

In contrast, Mrs. Diamante views her class as a place where language acquisition and learning math go hand in hand, where literacy supports math learning, where surprise is acknowledged and valued, where the thinking of others is recognized and appreciated, where making sense of math is more than a series of right and wrong answers. The physical arrangement of Mrs. Diamante's class supports small group work and face-to-face student interaction. Mrs. Diamante sees herself as a member of the mathematics community, in which reading, writing, risk taking, and sharing of ideas are necessary for a deep understanding of the concepts she will cover over the academic year. All students in Mrs. Diamante's class know that talking, reading, writing, and sharing ideas are essential to making sense of what they are learning. In other words, there is not separation among talking, reading, writing, sharing, and doing math in Mrs. Diamante's mathematics community of practice.

PARTICIPATION AND LEARNING MATH

The question to consider here is whether and to what extent were Marlena and other students acting, behaving, thinking, and taking part in goal-oriented, social activities that use language and literacy to further their involvement as members of mathematics communities of practice. Clearly much of what Mrs. Diamante did with students was for the sake of building background knowledge and familiarity with the mathematics register they would be using in subsequent units of study.

From the beginning, Mrs. Diamante engaged students in activities supported by physical and literacy-based learning. Her goal was to have students actively involved in constructing their understanding of plotting a point by having to learn the meaning of a point on a plane through multiple sources: visually and physically standing on the point, counting off positive and negative integers on x and y axes laid out on the tarp, plotting a point individually on a whiteboard graph, and writing about what they understood, noticed, found interesting, and made them wonder. To assist with vocabulary development and the appropriate use of symbols for talking and writing about the geometric relationships, Mrs. Diamante discussed the mathematical definitions and had students, working in pairs, write out their own definitions based on models of formal definitions she practiced with them. She shifted from using language that all students understood to the specific ways of talking about coordinates on plane, for example, changing up and down to rise and run. She talked about how difficult these words and ideas were for her when she was learning, and shared with students how she began to understand them.

The students were actively participating in ways that encouraged them to think about problems mathematically; namely, to think and share their thoughts about why and how concepts worked or didn't work to solve mathematical problems. This is what mathematicians do, and Mrs. Diamante was committed in practice to enabling active participation in mathematical ways of doing things. Mrs. Diamante was quite meticulous about going over concepts several times so that students had ample opportunities to participate in learning the meaning of the concepts. For example, several students had trouble remembering that a negative divided by a negative results in a positive number, meaning that the corresponding slope is also positive, moving from left to right. By having students actively engaged in building the slope on the tarp with string, in writing about it on their whiteboards and in their journals, and in discussions with their shoulder partners about it, Mrs. Diamante provides students with multiple means of engaging in mathematical practices.

WORKING TOGETHER TO LEARN MATH

Nearly all of the students in Mrs. Diamante's class were African American, Latino, or Native American; all 10 Latino students were English learners with various abilities in English. This ethnic and language composition of this class was fairly typical for the other math classes Mrs. D taught. Mrs. Diamante understood the importance of physically and socially integrating students of different ethnic backgrounds and different language and literacy abilities. She believed in a multiple abilities (Cohen, 1994) approach to participating in mathematical classroom practices. That is, all students have abilities that in combinations provide students with the tools they need to work on and figure out mathematical problems. For example, Tamika was really good at paying attention to details and writing them down. Marlena could memorize important concepts and procedures. Felipe was good at plotting points and lines on the graph. Together, these three students working together were able to participate in all the activities, and they helped one another to build their understanding of the various ideas and concepts being presented.

For students who are learning English, being in a small group that includes proficient English speakers enables them to hear proficient English being used conversationally as well as academically. In small group work focused on academic tasks, students ask guiding questions, repeat main ideas, and use genuine language that clarifies for English learners. These kinds of language uses, carried out in a here-and-now setting, provide English learners with the kinds of opportunities for hearing and using language that facilitate language acquisition. English learners are not only participating in mathematics, but also hearing, reading, and using language in ways that are aligned with how mathematicians interact in their communities of practice.

Mrs. Diamante was also aware that placing students in a small group was necessary, but insufficient for learning math. She emphasized to students that small group learning requires all students to participate through talk, listening, reading, and writing. Accordingly, while one group was writing on whiteboards, another was physically moving on the number line, and a third was working on specialized vocabulary tied to the activity. Mrs. Diamante organized each small group so that students of different abilities worked together in carrying out the tasks.

LANGUAGE IN MATH

It is not uncommon to hear that "mathematics is a language" (Whitin & Whitin, 2000). One reason people claim this is because mathematics uses a set of meaningful symbols to express ideas in conventional English syntax. Accordingly, $3 + 4 = 7$ and $3(5 X + 4) = 57$ can be read as English sentences: [three plus four equals the sum of seven]

PARTICIPATION STRATEGIES

There are three main participation structures you should use in your class: whole group teaching, small group learning, and individual learning. In whole group settings, you can pick name sticks out of a container to ensure that all students have an equal chance to participate. Organize small groups for optimal language and literacy ability differences. Experiment with different roles for each student. Have some students doing writing while others are involved in hands-on math activities. Make vocabulary development a high priority for every lesson.

Bibliography

Cantlon, T. (1991). *Structuring the classroom successfully for cooperative team learning.* Portland, OR: Prestige Publishers.

Cohen, E. (1994). *Designing groupwork: Strategies for the heterogeneous classroom.*
New York: Teachers College Press.

Kessler, C. (Ed.). (1992). *Cooperative language learning: A teacher's resource book.* Englewood Cliffs, NJ: Prentice Hall.

and [three times five X plus three times four equals fifty-seven] (where X = 3 and the distributive property is followed). However, equating mathematical syntax with A LANGUAGE is a misrepresentation. We reserve the term *language* for a meaningful communication system that is fundamentally socially based and passed on from caregivers (usually parents and other intimate adults) to children through culturally appropriate means (Heath, 1983; Ochs, 1988; Watson-Gegeo, 2004). However, math is language-based in the sense that is it often incomprehensible to those who don't "know" it. Moreover, you can argue that math has regional dialects, for example, different procedures for solving equations. Also, it is true that math is a socially constructed symbolic system of communicating ideas. Having said this, it is nonetheless true that math lacks a majority of the features inherent in human languages used for meaningful communication about emotions, desires, needs, and the past. A better way to understand how mathematics is language-based is to say that it is a *register*, a specialized way of expressing meaning that requires users to recognize and use vocabulary and expressions that can only be learned by participating in a particular community of practice. Registers are acquired in school settings and in settings where learners are apprenticed into the community of practice, where specialized vocabulary and expressions are meaningful only to group members. Parenthetically, language arts, social studies, and science are also academic registers.

In Mrs. Diamante's classroom, the register of math is embedded in social activities designed to enable students to try out and practice using mathematics in ways that correspond to how mathematicians solve mathematical problems. Mrs. Diamante integrates math concepts and mathematical language artfully so that students, regardless of their English language abilities, can participate in the activities and, in doing so, can eventually learn to think, act, and use language the way mathematicians do. She understands that students will vary in how well they are apprenticed into mathematics, that acquiring math takes repeated practice in ways of doing things with new vocabulary and expressions. For example, when the students move from plotting a point to plotting a line, they are doing more than substituting one noun phrase (a point) for another (a line). For students to conceptualize the difference between plotting a point and plotting a line, they need to participate in multiple activities, in which they talk, think, discuss, and write about what it means to do both activities. In other words, they need to practice the practices that apprentice them into using language in mathematically appropriate ways, language uses that align them with mathematics communities of practice. In Mrs. Diamante's class, students make meaning about math using oral and written language. Mrs. Diamante helps them understand how mathematical symbols and conventions are meaningful and useful as tools for learning about more advanced mathematical concepts and practices. Through continued engagement, discussion, and writing in which students use these basic concepts for meaningful purposes, they will be prepared for upcoming work on determining slope and solving real life slope-based problems.

GAINING A MATHEMATICS IDENTITY

One of Mrs. Diamante's primary goals in planning and carrying out mathematics activities is to ensure that students create and add on to their sociocultural identities that of being a mathematician. From day one, Mrs. Diamante talked with students about what it means to be mathematicians and how it involves talking and thinking about problems the way mathematicians might and do. Nowhere in Mrs. Diamante's activities are there messages about having to stop acting a certain way in order to take on a new identity. On the contrary, Mrs. Diamante

INTEGRATE LANGUAGE AND LITERACY INTO EVERYTHING YOU DO

You need to *think language* when you plan and carry out lessons with your students. Whenever possible, provide visual and written support for the concepts and ideas you want students to learn. Engage students in real conversations about what they are learning; have them write out what they understand and where they need additional work. Be a model for reading and writing about math concepts. Bring in art and music to support their learning.

Bibliography

The Help! Kit: A resource for secondary teachers of migrant English language learners. Available at www.escort.org.

Herrell, A., & Jordon, M. (2004). *Fifty strategies for teaching English language learners* (2nd ed.). Upper Saddle River, NJ: Merrill.

encourages students to use their home languages during small group work as needed to clarify mathematical register misunderstandings and to enhance understanding of concepts and ways of talking and thinking about mathematics. This approach to identity formation can be referred to as *acculturation without assimilation* (Gibson, 1988, 1997). In this manner, immigrant students engage in activities that add onto their existing identities without rejecting them and learn to move successfully between their multiple sociocultural and academic worlds.

Gaining an identity of a mathematician is a sociocultural process of becoming a member of mathematics communities of practice (Moschkovich, 2002). In the above episodes with Marlena and other students, Mrs. Diamante sets up activities so that students try out math concepts aligned with practices that existing mathematicians recognize and use for figuring out problems that involve slope. With practice, Marlena and the rest of the students will acquire the ways of using language and thinking about problems involving slope that are comparable to what mathematicians do in their communities of practices. This is not to say that all students in Mrs. Diamante's class will become full members of the mathematics community or that all students will take on identities as mathematicians with alacrity. Sometimes students choose to become a member; sometimes they need to be nudged and shown that they are capable of joining in and being successful. The point to stress is that Mrs. Diamante is inviting all students to become members of mathematics communities of practice and showing them how to talk and think about mathematics so that they have the opportunity to gain membership in the community.

Think about your own experiences with mathematics in high school and beyond. What sort of mathematics identity did you achieve in high school and college? In what ways did your teachers actively seek to invite you into the mathematics communities of practice or not? To those of you who are math teachers or working toward becoming math teachers, how strong is your identity affiliation with mathematics communities of practice, say, relative to how you see your identity as historians, physicists, or literati? Likewise, readers who are not members of the mathematics community, how do you see your identity as mathematicians compared to other sociocultural identities that together tie you to various communities of practice?

CONNECTING MATH TO WIDER CONTEXTS

One way to help students form math identities is to connect mathematics to real world practices in which the math concepts students are learning are essential for participation and problem solving. Successful math teachers connect classroom practices with real world practices (Whitin & Whitin, 2000). Math teachers who are successful with English learners know that connecting math with contexts that actively engage them in using oral and written language in the application of math concepts not only promotes academic language use, but also encourages math identity affiliation. Connecting math to

---

IDENTITY FORMATION AND LANGUAGE LEARNING

The following will help you learn more about the relationship between identity formation and language learning in school contexts.

Bibliography

Hawkins, M. R. (2004). Researching English language and literacy development in schools. *Educational Researcher, 33*(3), 14–25.

Lave, J., & Wenger, E. (1991). *Situated learning: Legitimate peripheral participation.* New York: Cambridge University Press.

Norton, B. (2000). *Identity and language learning: Gender, ethnicity and educational change.* Essex, England: Pearson Education.

students' surroundings can also promote social consciousness and enable students to reconsider the neutrality of mathematics discourse (Gutstein & Peterson, 2005).

Mathematics is both universal and highly contextual. It is universal in the sense that its principles are the same in any language, so that if the mathematical procedure is followed, the answer will always be the same. However, every math problem necessarily involves and is embedded in a social context, which a math teacher creates in order for students to learn the concepts and procedures. Accordingly, whether you are teaching ratios, probability, slope, or mean, mode, and median, there is always a social context for why and when students would use these concepts and procedures.

Many of you are undoubtedly familiar with some of the neutral ways of connecting math to social contexts. All of you have heard or attempted to solve story problems, such as the following:

> Cindy, age 15, Mark, age 14, and Jason, age 16, each contribute $6.00 to buy a large pizza that will be cut into 12 slices. How many slices are available for each person, and how much does each piece cost?

This story problem is seemingly neutral, but if you think about it, the story has several cultural features that mark it as mainstream, middle class: The persons' names, the food choice, and the fact that these youths each have $6.00 to spend on pizza. This story problem, therefore, connects to a social world of consumerism in which teenagers have spending money and enough food to share among them. For many immigrant English learners, this is a foreign cultural scene.

Okay, you might be thinking, how about if we change the problem set to Rosa, Marcos, and Miguel who all chip in $3.00 each to buy six enchiladas? In this case, immigrants from Mexico and other parts of Latin American might surely relate better to the story problem, but the implicit message about consumerism remains unquestioned as a way of life. Now, consider the following word problem:

> Teenage factory workers in Indonesia make 45 cents an hour sewing tennis shoes for an American company. They work 12 hours a day, 6 days a week. The company charges them $1.00 a day for food and water. How much do they earn per week, minus company fees?

This problem turns attention to economic globalism and the working conditions involved in producing popular commodities that many teenagers in the United States often take for granted (see Gutstein & Peterson, 2005). By connecting math to wider issues, you can help students see how understanding math can contribute to awareness about social justice. Such connections also give students the opportunity to raise important questions about needs of and practices in their surrounding communities (Zaslavsky, 1996).

Returning to Mrs. Diamante's classroom, throughout the lessons that prepare students for calculating slope, Mrs. D offers students opportunities to inquire about how slope might be useful for projects in their communities. She begins by asking students to look for slopes in parks, schools, and places where their families frequent for shopping. After students collect their ideas, she places them into small groups to brainstorm about the design of their projects, the kinds of support and materials they would need to build them, and how they would benefit the local community. In Marlena's group, the consensus was that they could design and build wheelchair ramps for the school basketball court and football stadium. Felipe's group decided on a skate ramp design for the community park near the school. Tamika and her group settled on a rain and sun shelter for nearby bus stops. Each group wrote up their design plans including slope calculations along with reasons for how the projects would improve existing conditions in their communities. When they were completed, each group sent their design plans to the appropriate agencies and groups to ask for their support in carrying out the projects.

CONNECTING MATH TO WIDER CONTEXTS

The following books will provide you with plenty of ideas for connecting math to wider contexts.

Bibliography

Darling-Hammond, L., French, J., & García-López, S. (Eds.). (2002). *Learning to teach for social justice.* New York: Teachers College Press.

Gutstein, E., & Peterson, B. (Eds.). (2005). *Rethinking mathematics: Teaching social justice by the numbers.* Milwaukee, WI: Rethinking Schools.

Zaslavsky, C. (1996). *The multicultural math classroom.* Portsmouth, NH: Heinemann.

MATH IN THE NATIVE LANGUAGE

Immigrant students and English learners who learned mathematics procedures and concepts in their native language and who gained identities as mathematicians in their native language are likely to use their native language for counting and arithmetic procedures (Cazden, 1986; Moschkovich, 2002). The use of the native language in learning academic content is compelling even when the policies and assumptions argue against it (Lucas & Katz, 1994). Among immigrant students with parallel schooling experiences who are still learning English, relying on the native language for discussion of concepts and procedures during small group work enables these students to participate in and benefit from the activities. For students who are struggling in math because of gaps in their knowledge, having a team member who can explain concepts and procedures in a language they understand provides access to the academic content, and it enables the students to continue their studies in a content area that is critical for graduating high school and for gaining entrance to college.

Teachers who are proficient in the students' native language can use their abilities to have additional access to classroom activities and content area knowledge. They can preview and review main ideas to check for understanding and to assess the extent to which further scaffolding is needed. They can also maintain a classroom library of native language resources—bilingual dictionaries, materials in the native language, and textbooks in the native language.

Summary

In this chapter, we have shown how English learners can participate actively in challenging mathematics classes, with a teacher who is committed to ensuring their participation and identity formation as mathematicians. Mrs. Diamante is such a teacher. To create a dynamic community of practice in her math class, Mrs. D took the following steps:

- She guided her students through a series of activities that integrated language, literacy, and mathematics concepts so that as students learned math, they also gained proficiency in English.
- She enabled students to discuss what they were learning in the native language if they wanted, and as much as possible, English learners worked alongside fully English proficient students, exchanging and clarifying ideas in English.

- She provided students with multiple means of engaging in mathematical practices so that they were hearing, reading, and using language in ways that are aligned with how mathematicians interact in their communities of practice, thus giving her students the opportunity to gain membership into broader communities of practice in mathematics.

- She engaged students in activities that added onto their existing identities without rejecting them. She helped them to move successfully between their multiple sociocultural and academic worlds.

- Together students developed projects that contributed to their mathematics and English learning, as well as to the idea that mathematics can be a powerful tool for investing in their surrounding communities.

As English learners in Mrs. Diamante's class become apprenticed into mathematics as a community of practice, they will grow in their English ability as well as their ability to interact within the academic discourse of mathematics. Teachers who structure their classrooms as Mrs. Diamante has will find that their English learners can have access to higher levels of mathematical practices than English learners who sit in traditional classrooms, row by row, listening to the teacher lecture.

Activities

1. Think back to your high school days and describe the best and worst math teachers for students who did not identify well with mathematics practices. What did these teachers do to try to invite reluctant learners into mathematics?

2. Divide the class into various academic content areas and form groups of 3 to 4 students per group. In each group, list and describe ways of being, thinking, believing, and acting that you consider to be specific to mathematics communities of practice.

3. Select a mathematics concept taught in high school algebra that you consider to be highly abstract. Explain how you would teach the concept so that English learners would be able to (a) participate in the lesson, (b) exchange ideas with other students, (c) learn English while they studied the concept, (d) act in ways that support mathematics identities, and (e) connect what they are learning to real world context.

4. Search the Internet for math units appropriate to your grade level and area of interest. Review the extent to which the unit connects to real world contexts and social justice issues. What would you propose to make units relevant to social justice issues?

5. Interview at least two high school math teachers about what they do to invite English learners to participate in and benefit from math learning activities. Ask how they select materials and how they make connections to real world issues and practices.

References

Cazden, C. (1986). Classroom discourse. In M. C. Wittrock (Ed.), *Handbook of research in teaching* (3rd ed., pp. 432–463). New York: Macmillan.

Cohen, E. (1994). *Designing groupwork: Strategies for the heterogeneous classroom.* New York: Teachers College Press.

Gibson, M. (1997). Complicating the immigrant/involuntary minority typology. *Anthropology & Education Quarterly, 28*(3), 431-454.

Gibson, M. (1988). *Accommodation without assimilation: Sikh immigrants in an American high school.* Ithaca, NY: Cornell University Press.

Gutstein, E., & Peterson, B. (Eds.). (2005). *Rethinking mathematics: Teaching social justice by the numbers.* Milwaukee, WI: Rethinking Schools.

Heath, S. B. (1983). *Ways with words.* New York: Cambridge University Press.

Lucas, T., & Katz, A. (1994). Reframing the debate: The roles of native languages in English-only programs for language minority students. *TESOL Quarterly, 28*(4), 537–562.

Moschkovich, J. (2002). A situated and sociocultural perspective on bilingual mathematics learners. *Mathematical Thinking and Learning, 4*(2&3), 189–212.

Ochs, E. (1988). *Culture and language development: Language acquisition and language socialization in a Samoan village.* New York: Cambridge University Press.

Watson-Gegeo, K. (2004). Mind, language, and epistemology: Toward a language socialization paradigm for SLA. *Modern Language Journal, 88*(3), 331–350.

Whitin, P., & Whitin, D. (2000). *Math is language too: Talking and writing in the mathematics classroom.* Urbana, IL: National Council of Teachers of English.

Zaslavsky, C. (1996). *The multicultural math classroom: Bringing in the world.* Portsmouth, NH: Heinemann.

6

Communities of Practice in the Social Studies Classroom

Anne Vega/Merrill

ISABELA'S CLASS

Isabela looked up from her writing and looked out the window. How sad this story was! Isabela looked again at the picture of Cherokee Indians, huddled against the cold as they walked their way westward in what was called the "Trail of Tears." She was working with a small group on an inquiry project as part of the westward expansion unit her U.S. History class was doing. She had decided to write a journal from the perspective of a young Cherokee girl who was forced from her lands in the Indian Removal Act of 1838. Although she was learning a lot by doing the project, writing the journal was really affecting her. For the first time, she realized what it would be like to be taken from your home and forced to march in the winter for 800 miles to an unknown place. Initially, Isabela couldn't believe what she was reading. How could something like this have happened less than 200 years earlier? She had pondered her own forced move from Mexico two years before. She hadn't wanted to come to the United States, and she thought of her move as the "Isabela Removal Act" after she first learned about the Trail of Tears. But then Isabela realized that her family had chosen to move, even if she hadn't, whereas the Cherokee had been brutally forced from their homes. Her disbelief had slowly given way to anger. She started to understand what her teacher, Ms. Grijalva, called "basic human rights." The Indian Removal Act was a violation of basic human rights. As she learned more and more about the Cherokee, and as she imagined a real Cherokee girl being marched hundreds of miles in the cold of winter, her anger turned into a profound sense of sadness. It surprised her that a history class could have this kind of effect on her.

Isabela realized as she wrote that if 4,000 of 16,000 total Cherokee died on the march that meant one out of every four. It was very likely that her fictional character, a 15-year-old girl, would have lost at least one family member. She decided that she would have to include that in her journal.

Ms. Grijalva let them do a lot of group projects in class. Most of the time, she picked groups for the projects so that they would learn to work together, as she said. In the beginning, Isabela didn't like having groups picked for her. But as she got to know more students in the class, she felt more and more comfortable working with them. Ms. Grijalva always seemed to pick kids who could do different kinds of things, and that helped them with their projects.

For the westward expansion unit, as with other units they had worked on, Ms. Grijalva gave them choices about what to study. Ms. Grijalva was required to use the textbook, but she didn't like it very much. She said it didn't include enough information. So what she did was take the time period and pull out the most important dates and events from the unit. She included these on a "Key

Words and Events" handout that she gave each member of the class. Each group would try to find how their topic related to the key words and events from the list as they did their projects. Isabela also had a reflection log, a spiral notebook in which she wrote new words, events, and journal responses that she wrote on her own or that were assigned. Ms. Grijalva looked at her reflection log at different times to make sure Isabela was progressing in her learning. At the beginning of the year, Isabela wrote a lot in Spanish. Now she was writing more and more in English.

Students chose whatever project they wanted to do. Ms. Grijalva always gave them a list of ideas and talked a little about each of them, but the groups could decide on a different topic, if they wanted to, as long as it was within the same time period. During the year, students had studied history through the music of the times, through art, through minority voices, and through many other perspectives than just the textbook. Each group read the textbook chapters to see how the book covered their topic, and then discussed and explored why they felt the book included some information and not other information. That way, they "covered" the information from the textbook, but they also learned a whole lot more. After every group had presented their project, Ms. Grijalva spent a couple of class periods "making connections" between the topics and "contextualizing" them in the times. This time a group was going to do the "making connections" part as their project. Isabela looked forward to that part. She understood her own topic more when she saw how it fit together with other events. The class was like a puzzle, she thought, and she was an important piece in it. Every piece had equal importance to the whole picture.

The final part of the unit would be a group discussion, in which they would look at current events and attitudes and try to tie them to historical events and attitudes. Once they started their projects, they often found newspaper articles and news stories on related events, and they shared these with the class on an ongoing basis.

Isabela never spoke during whole group discussions. She felt too shy, though she thought she might try it some time. But Ms. Grijalva always started whole group discussions with a fast-write or a small group sharing time, with members from different groups than their inquiry groups so they could learn more about different events that happened during the same time period. Isabela felt more comfortable sharing in small groups, so she always felt like she was a part of the discussion. Isabela couldn't say that she felt like she belonged in every class, and she was happy that she felt comfortable in her history class. And she was learning a lot.

Her group included David, Luís, Jessica, and herself. Two of them were White and spoke English as their first language. Luís was from Central Mexico, like Isabela. When they got together for the first time and looked over the list of topics for the Westward Expansion unit, the "Indian Removal Act" caught their eye. Ms. Grijalva had taught them about how Native Americans were treated in

U.S. history. Isabela remembered a lot of the history she had learned in Mexico about the native people there, especially during the time of the *conquistadores*. She was curious to know how the United States and Mexico compared with how they had treated Indians over time. Luís knew some things about that, too, and so they had decided to do their project on the Trail of Tears. As a part of their project, they were going to present some of the information they already knew about Mexican history and how it related to U.S. history in a Venn diagram.

They had worked together on developing a timeline and had already found connections to almost all of the terms on the Key Words and Events list. Because Luís knew how to use the Internet, he researched many of the terms online. David liked to write about historical events, so he did major parts of the writing, and Jessica helped organize the whole project. She was also in charge of the presentation. Isabela had gathered the pictures and visuals for the project, and she was also writing the journal. Since her written English wasn't as good as David's, he would edit it after she wrote a rough draft. Ms. Grijalva helped Isabel with her English, as well. They had spent a lot of time talking and planning for the project. They had little group meetings at the beginning of each class period to discuss what they had found and accomplished. In one of those meetings, Luís had told about a story he found in which a woman on the Trail of Tears had given her blanket to a young boy who was shivering. The boy ended up dying because the blanket had diseases on it. When they did more research, they discovered that some soldiers actually gave diseased blankets on purpose so that more Indians would die. They decided that it was important to include a section on hardships and sicknesses on the Trail of Tears. Then Isabela had an idea that they should also include a section on ways that the U.S. government had purposefully tried conceal to the American public that soldiers were killing Indian men, women, and children. Jessica said it was a great idea, because so many Americans had protested the Indian Removal Act, and maybe there were other stories like that. They became really excited, and Luís went online to see what he could find. They felt like investigators, trying to figure out some great mysteries. And they found out some amazing things.

The final part of the inquiry project would be a community action project. Isabela, Luís, Jessica, and David had already decided that they would write a letter of opinion to their state and federal legislators. Isabela had some notes in her reflection log of things she'd like to say in the letter. She hoped the congressional representatives would read the letter and maybe even write back.

But today all of their discoveries just made Isabela sad. She decided to name her character "Quanti" after the wife of Chief John Ross, who perished on the trail. Thoughts of Quanti stayed with her throughout the day as she pondered the hardships real people endured. What would it be like to be Quanti, to be forced from your home? What would it be like to watch as your grandmother or little sister weakened, grew sick, and died in the cold? How could you walk away from their bodies, not knowing how they would be cared for? How would your feet keep moving through the cold snow, and how would your heart keep beating even as it was breaking?

Isabela had even shed a few tears of her own as she thought about it. It was Luís who brought her the most comfort. One day, he handed Isabela a picture of flower. "It's a Cherokee Rose," he said. Isabela looked at the flower, and then read the story underneath the picture, called "The Legend of the Cherokee Rose." She read that the Cherokee women shed many tears on the Trail of Tears. Chief John Ross, seeing all the sadness, prayed that something good would come out of it. As the legend goes, after he prayed, each time a woman shed a tear, a beautiful white rose would grow where the tear fell. Even today, along the historical path of the Trail of Tears, hundreds of Cherokee Roses still grow. Isabela looked up at Luís and smiled. "Thank you so much," she said. He nodded and quickly walked away. Isabela decided right then and there that she would make a drawing for their project. It would be of Quanti, tears rolling down her cheeks. Beneath her feet, and the ground below her, she would draw big Cherokee Roses, beautiful and white, and full of hope.

COMMITMENTS IN PRACTICE IN ISABELA'S CLASSROOM

Generally speaking, social studies classes provide many opportunities for including English learners. Indeed, English learners who come from different parts and perspectives of the world are well-equipped to contribute their background knowledge and experiences to the class community. Everyone benefits. Social studies teachers are finding that they can easily teach within federal, state, and district guidelines by covering periods of history through inquiry projects, primary sources, and other activities that go beyond traditional basal readers. History can be brought to life in the classroom in communities of practice that are active, engaged, and passionate about learning how the world works and has worked over time. For this to happen, however, teachers need to move away from the traditional read-the-chapter-answer-the-questions-take-the-test format. Isabela's classroom shows how teachers can set up the social studies classroom in ways that promote our commitments in practice. Below we discuss how each commitment is reflected in Isabela's classroom.

STUDYING THE WORLD BY DOING SOCIAL STUDIES

Traditional read-the-chapter-answer-the-questions-take-the-test social studies programs are detrimental to English learners as well as traditional mainstream students (Freeman, Freeman, & Mercuri, 2002). Such approaches rely heavily on texts and ways of using language that usually make the material inaccessible to most English learners. In addition, this approach promotes rote memorization over deeper understandings. Students often memorize facts for the tests and then promptly forget the information.

Ms. Grijalva promoted active participation in Isabela's class through the inquiry-based projects. Ms. Grijalva was able to include all of the state and district content standards by helping students make connections to them through their own inquiry. As with Ms. Pherson's class in the language arts chapter, Ms. Grijalva encouraged active participation in her class by including the elements of choice, voice, responsibility, and contribution. Isabela was able to choose which topic to explore with her group and was a part of decision making throughout the inquiry project. Along with each group member, Isabela took on specific responsibilities within the group, according to her strengths. She was able to contribute through her own unique gifts: her knowledge of Mexican history, her artistic abilities, and her sense of empathy with the Cherokee.

Ms. Grijalva chose group members according to these strengths. However, such groupings can't just be formed and left to chance (Cohen, 1994). To ensure that the group continued to work well together, Ms. Grijalva had them schedule regular planning meetings. She sat in on the meetings when possible and also followed up with individual responsibilities through conferences. Group cohesion is very important to active participation, and so the teacher must monitor it. But it is a reciprocal process, as students must also hold themselves accountable for their part of the project. Here again, Ms. Grijalva plays a role. If a task is too difficult for a student, Ms. Grijalva can fill in the gaps and offer that student individual support. In this way, active participation and contribution are both supported.

Active participation can't happen if students feel anxious that their contributions will not be adequate. It is paramount that the class promote a risk-free environment in which students are able to make suggestions and make mistakes. Failure is an integral part of learning, and the teacher must set the tone for process learning. This kind of environment is inclusive to all (Spaulding, Carolino, & Amen, 2004).

SOCIAL INTEGRATION FOR LANGUAGE AND CONTENT LEARNING

As we've stated before, social integration is paramount for all learners. Since learning is largely social (Faltis, 2006; Hawkins, 2004; Lave & Wenger, 1991), community members must have the opportunity to learn through interdependent relationships. Heterogeneous groupings are an integral part of social integration (Cohen, 1994). In Isabela's class, Ms. Grijalva made sure to mix students as often as possible. Therefore, she often chose groups for the students based on what she knew of each student's strengths. Isabela's group worked well together. As native English speakers, David and Jessica contributed by taking on the writing and presenting aspects of the inquiry project (though language is certainly not the only strength required for writing and presenting). However, Luís's computer abilities were vital for the research aspect of the project. Isabela's unique ability to empathize caused her to suggest the journal piece of the project. That, in turn, revitalized their interests and caused them to do more research. Both Luís and Isabela were able to contribute, and both were immersed in the language of social studies through talk and written language.

The teacher must also give students opportunities to work on their learning needs. Therefore, Ms. Grijalva will need to find other classroom opportunities for students to take on roles that purposefully allow them to grow in specific areas. David and Jessica need to grow in their research skills and in their ability to empathize, just as Luís and Isabela need to grow in their written and spoken English. It will fall to Ms. Grijalva to organize and make explicit these opportunities for growth. Ms. Grijalva occasionally will allow students to pick their own groups, especially when there is a particular area of interest they'd like to explore together. However, Ms. Grijalva has seen that it is easy for cliques to form in classrooms, and she always keeps an eye on the social relations among her students. She discusses the health of the classroom community with the students in order to solicit their contributions to a healthy interdependent community.

Isabela was able to integrate with other class members through multiple small group and large group activities. When Ms. Grijalva had large group discussions, she reduced the language demands for English learners through think-pair-share activities, free-writes, and small group sharing activities. She broke groups up and created new groups within units of instruction so that they might teach one another. In this way, every student becomes an expert and a teacher of their particular topic of study. Isabela was still too shy to speak up in large group, but small groupings allowed her to interact around the content and within the community. She hoped to speak up more in whole class discussions in the future.

Classroom communities that foster individual growth within interdependent relationships are both rigorous and rewarding. Ms. Grijalva has to think way beyond content standards to create this kind of community of practice. However, the benefits of such foresight and planning are immense.

LANGUAGE LEARNING IN AND THROUGH SOCIAL STUDIES

In Isabela's class, language was used to mediate content learning. Ms. Grijalva set up multiple and varied opportunities for the students to engage in content through language. In other words, Isabela and her classmates had opportunities to read, write about, and discuss historical events in large and small groups and individually. To scaffold the specific language and historical concepts Ms. Grijalva wanted the students to learn during the course of the unit, she gave them a handout with guiding words and concepts for them to connect to their individual project. Further, Ms. Grijalva had each student keep a learning log in which they would write notes, make lists of new words and events, and write journal responses in various in-class activities. Ms. Grijalva monitored these learning logs throughout the year, using them for assessment and to guide instruction. She then allowed her students to explore the topics of their choice through various means so that students could rely on their strengths and interests to explore and discover historical events from primary sources, secondary sources, and group discussions.

To scaffold this process for all of her learners, Ms. Grijalva scheduled meetings with each group so that she could monitor their progress on their ongoing research project. Through these guided meetings, Ms. Grijalva could assess the skills each student was acquiring and monitor their progress on the discourse and content of history. Further, Ms. Grijalva could assess which students would benefit from one-on-one conferences that would help them fulfill their role in the small group project. These guided meetings and individual conferences were places where Isabela and others could get additional oral and written language and academic support. They also ensured that Isabela could contribute to the small group inquiry project and the larger class as a whole.

Jigsaws, think-pair-shares, fast-writes, and scaffolded small-group-into-large-group discussions provided various venues for content-based discussion (Short, 1993). Further, each student had a role in researching and presenting historical events for both small and large groups. All these activities and interactions helped to integrate language support with content.

SOCIOCULTURAL IDENTITY SUPPORT

Inquiry projects such as the one Ms. Grijalva facilitated are based in choice and interest. When students are able to choose topics based on interest, they will likely draw from prior knowledge and experiences that are based in their individual sociocultural identity. Isabela had some knowledge of the history of people indigenous to Mexico. She also could identify with being forced to move to a new home. Thus, her choice of working on the Indian Removal Act was based in her own sociocultural identity. Ms. Grijalva must encourage students to draw from their prior knowledge and experiences to add a creative edge to their inquiry, such as Isabela's journal and the Venn diagram Isabela and Luís planned to make comparing Mexican and U.S. treatment of indigenous peoples. Ms. Grijalva will have to play an active role in this by both knowing her students well and knowing history well. By knowing her students, she can find ways to make connections to their present-day lives and events in history. By knowing history, she can match areas of interest to her students.

Further, Ms. Grijalva must be open to different kinds of information and presentation that may be based in sociocultural affiliations much different from her own (including, as we all know, generational differences). For example, if students want to perform a rap song about the Trail of Tears, Ms. Grijalva needs to be open to such a presentation while still holding the students to a reliance on historical accuracy (based in evidence) in their song. Ms. Grijalva will need to work with the whole class in encouraging them to value different approaches to information and learning.

Part of sociocultural identity formation involves taking on new ways of thinking, doing, understanding, and being based on participation in new communities of practice. By organizing social studies around inquiry-based projects, and inviting students to see themselves as historians and social scientists who study the past, Ms. Grijalva also apprenticed Isabela, Jessica, Luís, and the other students into social studies communities. In short, by doing history her students became historians.

In short, strengthening and nurturing different language and cultural identities and affinities in the social studies classroom is a multifaceted task. Teachers must actively work toward inclusion and a sense of belonging for every student, and at the same time, work toward helping students form new identities as social scientists. The classroom community must learn to stretch and grow as it welcomes new ways of thinking and behaving, ways that are aligned with social studies communities of practice. Furthermore, teachers must be knowledgeable about history beyond the traditional European-American perspective (Banks, 2004). They must be historians and teachers: knowledgeable, caring, and thoughtful in how they help create the classroom community of practice.

WEAVING THE PAST INTO CURRENT EVENTS

Social studies classrooms are fecund environments for exploring issues of social justice both in the past and present. In Isabela's class, her small group explored the events that led up to and followed the Indian Removal Act of 1838. Although the Trail of Tears is often mentioned in history basals, it is often glossed over or construed as one isolated event, when in fact it was one event of many in which native peoples were subjected to cruelty and oppression, what in today's terms might be called terrorism. Isabela and her group were able to connect to wider contexts by having the opportunity to explore this one event in more detail. The students in Isabela's class worked with alacrity to connect events within the same time period and then to tie them into contemporary events. As Isabela and her group found current newspaper articles and explored issues relevant to land rights of Native American peoples, they were exploring modern day issues of social justice. Further, Luís and Isabela were able to add to these explorations through their knowledge of indigenous peoples of Mexico and how the Mexican government has treated them over time. Small and large group discussions surrounding westward expansion helped the class as a whole see who the players were in those times and who benefited from which actions. Looking together at the big picture helps students recognize wider contexts within their content areas and beyond.

Finally, each group had to generate a community action project as a result of their study. Isabela's group chose to write a letter to their representatives in both state and federal congress to express their informed opinions about how Native Americans were treated historically and continue to be treated in present times. Such a letter may or may not reflect a large amount of agency, but the result is that the students connect to their imagined communities of practice as they practice becoming citizens of our democracy.

In our experience, secondary students flourish when they get a sense of their own agency both inside and beyond school. When this sense of agency is tied to knowledge of history, politics, demographics, and issues of social justice, these students become well-informed citizens of our world.

A LOOK AT STUDENTS NEW TO ENGLISH

Students who are new to English benefit from an inquiry-based social studies program because choice allows them to draw from their unique knowledge and experience to access new content and language. English learners in Ms. Grijalva's classroom are scaffolded into U.S. history by relying on their strengths to contribute and learn from others. As students who are new to English work in their zones of proximal development, more capable peers, as well as the teacher, help support their English language growth through group interactions around content (Wink & Putney, 2001). Further, the teacher provides additional support through one-on-one conferences in which she gives direct instruction on applying new vocabulary and concepts in context of content-based inquiry. English learners, along with other students in the class, keep a learning log that includes relevant vocabulary and concepts that are both individualized and content based. Ms. Grijalva's work in conferences and her ongoing assessments of Isabela's abilities allow her to guide instruction toward meeting Isabela's and others' needs. In the meantime, Isabela is not segregated from the class community, nor is she held back until she learns enough vocabulary. She learns vocabulary and concepts within content-based instruction, integrated with the class.

The key point for Isabela and other English learners in Ms. Grijalva's class is that they are an integral part of the community from day one. Isabela has choices, contributes, and benefits from small and large group interactions. All of this is scaffolded through one-on-one interactions with the teacher who keeps a constant eye on the give-and-take of the relationships within the class community. Such scaffolded interactions bring all learners into a community of practice, and all learners reap the benefits.

STUDENTS WITH NONPARALLEL SCHOOLING EXPERIENCES

Many times students who have gaps in their schooling or even no schooling at all enroll in our classes. Students who come to us from nonparallel schooling experiences are not *without* knowledge (a deficit model), but they do come to us with a rich knowledge base in other, outside school areas. Students who arrive in social studies classrooms with nonparallel schooling experiences will benefit from a structure that allows the teacher some one-on-one conferences or guided group interactions. Students with different ability levels can be expected to contribute to the classroom community of practice, and the teacher can support such contributions. Students will contribute according to their current and growing abilities. As their abilities grow the nature of their contributions changes, becoming less contextualized and more linguistic. However, we believe that all students can contribute and benefit from communities of practice that meet the needs of all learners. In an inclusive and supportive environment, students with nontraditional backgrounds will quickly learn school-based norms of interaction while at the same time contributing to the knowledge of their classmates. We must know our students' backgrounds and understand their strengths so that we can scaffold mutually beneficial academic relationships.

THE ROLE OF NATIVE LANGUAGE

As with all content areas, native language is paramount for English learners in social studies classes. In some states, laws preclude bilingual teachers from instructing in a native language. At the same time, more and more classrooms are filling up with diverse populations representing many different languages. Because of increasingly limiting laws and growing language diversity in today's classrooms, it is becoming more and more difficult for teachers to use native language in either formal or informal instruction. However, in our experience, even states with the strictest English-only laws allow students to navigate new information in their native language. The Internet provides endless research possibilities in multiple languages, and books are printed and translated internationally. Teachers in social studies classrooms should make an extra effort to find materials in the native language of their students. When students can rely on prior knowledge, including linguistic knowledge, to navigate new content, they have greater access to content-based concepts and language in English.

Teachers can use native language in many ways to help students gain access to discursive properties and conceptual knowledge within content areas, even when the teacher doesn't speak the native languages of some or all of the students. A short list is included in the following box.

Native language is an important tool in accessing content and vocabulary in English. Native language can be used to scaffold a student's entry into communities of practice whose linguistic norm is English. Regular classroom teachers will find that multiple sources in multiple languages give access not only to English learners being invited into communities of practice, but also to multiple perspectives

---

NATIVE LANGUAGE IN THE SOCIAL STUDIES CLASSROOM

1. Students can gain access to content knowledge through Internet sources, books, magazines, and newspapers that are printed in their own language.
2. Students can use native language in learning logs for clarification of vocabulary or concepts.
3. Students can write in native language, and then translate into English, thus gaining access to concepts first, language second (a whole-to-part model).
4. Students can discuss concepts with classmates from the same or similar linguistic backgrounds in their native language.
5. Students can share knowledge with their classmates in their native language, and then paraphrase it in English for classmates.
6. Students can write down and reflect on new knowledge in learning logs in the native, the target language, or both.

surrounding social studies topics. Native language is a powerful tool for English learners in social studies classrooms.

Summary

All students can and must have the opportunity to contribute to social studies classrooms. Some of the ways that Ms. Grijalva apprenticed her students into her classroom community of practice follow:

- She promoted active participation through inquiry-based projects, building in elements of choice, voice, responsibility, and contribution.
- She encouraged process learning within a risk-free environment.
- She created heterogeneous groupings such that students could work together, drawing from each others' strengths.
- Academic language and content were integrated within various large and small group activities. Think-pair-shares, fast-writes, learning logs, and jigsaws helped mediate individual learning within the larger community. Ms. Grijalva focused on academic language *in context* of content-based activities, all based in student interest.
- Inquiry-based projects invited students to see themselves as historians and social scientists who study the past. By strengthening and nurturing different language and cultural identities and affinities in her classroom, Ms. Grijalva apprenticed her students into a classroom community of practicing historians.
- Community action projects allowed students to recognize wider contexts within their content areas and beyond. Exploring issues of social justice helped students get a sense of agency both inside and beyond school. This agency, when tied to knowledge of politics, history, demographics, and social justice, helps students become well-informed citizens of our world.

When we as teachers create opportunities for community interactions around content, we must consider how we can structure our classrooms such that everyone benefits, and everyone contributes. The possibilities in such classrooms are endless and rewarding.

Activities

1. History textbooks often privilege a hegemonic view of historical events. Pick a time period or unit and do some library research to find additional sources, including primary sources and sources that reflect alternative perspectives.

2. Find an adult immigrant who is well-versed in history. Conduct an interview to find what he or she was taught regarding a specific historical event. What are the differences and similarities of what he or she was taught versus what you were taught?

3. Plan a social studies unit without using the basal textbook (except as a reference). Avoid worksheets and texts. Based on the kinds of practices mentioned in this chapter, what kind of learning activities in the basal do you think will support English learners?

4. In most secondary social studies classrooms the teacher controls the class curriculum (in compliance with district and state guidelines). What are some ways to give more curricular decisions to students?

5. How can you support English learners and students with nonparallel schooling experiences in gaining access to secondary social studies communities of practice? Give specific examples.

6. Pick a unit of study from a social studies classroom and explore ways you can help students make connections to wider contexts. What kinds of social justice action projects can be added to the unit to help students identify with imagined communities of practice?

References

Banks, J. (2004). Multicultural education: Historical development, dimensions, and practice. In J. Banks & C. McGee Banks (Eds.), *Handbook of research on multicultural education* (pp. 3–29). San Francisco, CA: Jossey-Bass.

Cohen, E. (1994). *Designing groupwork: Strategies for the heterogeneous classroom.* New York: Teachers College Press.

Faltis, C. (2006). *Teaching English language learners in elementary school communities: A join-fostering approach.* Upper Saddle River, NJ: Merrill.

Freeman, Y., Freeman, D., & Mercuri, S. (2002). *Closing the achievement gap: How to reach limited-formal-schooling and long-term English learners.* Portsmouth, NH: Heinemann.

Hawkins, M. R. (2004). Researching English language and literacy development in schools. *Educational Researcher, 33*(3), 14–25.

Lave, J., & Wenger, E. (1991). *Situated learning: Legitimate peripheral participation.* New York: Cambridge University Press.

Short, D. (1993). *Integrating language and culture in middle school American history classes.* Washington, DC: Center for Applied Linguistics.

Spaulding, S., Carolino, B., & Amen, K. (2004). *Immigrant students and secondary school reform: Compendium of best practices.* Washington, DC: Council of State Chief School Officers.

Wink, J., & Putney, L. (2001). *A vision of Vygotsky.* Boston: Allyn & Bacon.

Physics for English Learners: You Want Us to Push What?

Tom Watson/Merrill

VICENTE'S CLASS

Mr. Morrison had a big grin on his face. Today was the day he had been building up to for weeks. Sixteen-year-old Vicente Pájaro knew something was up because Mr. Morrison was wearing his old lab coat. That was usually a sign that the class was going to begin a new experiment. Vicente adjusted his glasses, looking about the classroom for clues of what was to come. Mr. Morrison was carrying a clipboard in one hand and a box of stopwatches in the other, waiting for the bell to ring.

Vicente always sat in the front of the class because, even with glasses, he couldn't see that well, and he loved this class—Physics. He had not always been so enthused about the class; in fact, when his counselor enrolled him after 2 years at Ferris High School, an urban school of nearly 2,000 students, where the majority of students were Hispanic and English learners, he was terrified to take the class. Coming straight from Morelia, Michoacan, in Mexico, Vicente had passed all of the English language development courses offered by the school, and although he still struggled with English literacy, he was drawn toward math and science because as he says, "Is no so hard for me to do thins I can see in front of me." Still, everybody at Ferris knew that physics was hard, even with Mr. Morrison, who was considered to be one of the best teachers there.

Vicente was 1 of 4 English learners in Mr. Morrison's class of 24 students. Half of the other students were Chicanos, some of whom were bilingual, and the rest were White students. There were 7 girls in the class, all of whom were English speakers. Mr. Morrison lived and breathed physics. His home, within walking distance from the school, was cluttered with materials, games, and equipment that he had accumulated over his 15 years as a physics teacher at Ferris High. When Mr. Morrison began teaching at Ferris, the school was predominately White, but over time as Mexican families moved into the surrounding communities, and White families moved out, the school changed into a predominately Hispanic high school. Mr. Morrison welcomed the changing demographics, but knew that he had to expand his teaching knowledge if he were to be successful with students who were learning English while they were also grappling with physics. He read and took classes at the local university on methods of teaching English as a second language, the nature of language, and sheltered content teaching. After several years of teaching English learners, he devised his own formula for success:

Mr. Morrison's Rule

$$HELP = (L + H) + (S - L)$$

In this equation, Mr. Morrison defined HELP, Helping English Learners in Physics, as a function of [language support plus hands-on practices] coupled with [small group work and minimal lectures to the whole class], with scalar quantity measured in the ability to show learning by using physics language and do physics activities as they are done in physics communities of practice.

From the first week of class, Mr. Morrison made sure that every concept he presented followed this rule. As a result, Vicente and the other English learners had been successful in staying with the class, not only learning new vocabulary, but also participating in the activities that incorporated the concepts that at first had seemed far beyond their grasp. In the weeks leading up to today, Vicente had learned to talk and write about key physics ideas related to force, motion, acceleration, velocity, and displacement. He had worked in small groups using motion maps to figure out the position, velocity, and acceleration of an object for a given time interval. He and his team members had to figure out whether the velocity of the object in motion was constant, positive, or negative, and be able to represent graphically the velocity vectors for various velocity patterns.

But even before filling out the motions maps, Vicente participated in the Stomper Car experiment, which examined the motion of a miniature car and determined its velocity through a series of observable and measurable tests using the following calculations:

$$V_{ave} = \frac{X_2 - X_1}{t_2 - t_1} \qquad a_{ave} = \frac{v_2 - v_1}{t_2 - t_1}$$

In Vicente's group, Vicente had the job of putting down a small washer to mark where the front of the car was each time the timer called out 2 seconds. Phillip Nembé, from Cameroon, was the timer, and Marsha was in charge of winding up the car and placing it on the ground 30 centimeters from the starting point. Once the experiment was completed and the data analyzed, Mr. Morrison asked all the groups to come up with questions about velocity and acceleration. Because they had taken good notes before and during the experiment, Phillip, Marsha, and Vicente were able to generate three questions, and they checked their calculations to make sure that they had the right answers before sharing them with Mr. Morrison and the entire class.

For the next activity, Mr. Morrison asked the entire class, "Have you ever been standing by the street when a car zooms by and you ask yourself 'Man, how fast was that car going?' After today, you should be able to figure out just how fast the car was going." Vicente was intrigued because this was the first time the class was going to apply physics to find out something useful. Since he had already worked with the concept of velocity in the Stomper Car experiment, when Mr. Morrison reminded the class that velocity was also change in displacement over change in time, Vicente had little trouble grasping what he had to do to calculate the speed of a passing car. After several attempts, his group was able to pinpoint the speed in miles per second, kilometers per hour, and miles per hour.

Now, the day had come for the final experiment. When the class had settled down, Mr. Morrison reviewed the main vocabulary and concepts up to that point. He had prepared vocabulary cards with words and formulae and asked individual students to explain them by acting them out. Once this was completed, Mr. Morrison stood in front of the class for a few seconds, smiling and rubbing his hands together. He picked up a box of stopwatches and calmly said, "Today, I want you to follow me to the parking lot so you can push my Ford Explorer Sport Trac using only two bathroom scales. Your goal is to find the mass of my truck."

"You want us to push what?" asked Vicente, bewildered. "Is impossible with yust two escales. Is too heavy," he added, looking around the class for support.

Phillip's hand shot up and Mr. Morrison called on him. "I am not understanding. You want the student to push the car with something? I don't know what is the batroom scale."

"Here, let me show you what a bathroom scale is," replied Mr. Morrison slowly and clearly as he walked over to his desk to retrieve the two scales. "Come here, Phillip, stand on this scale and tell the class how much you weigh." The class giggled as Phillip, who stood nearly 6 feet tall, announced that he weighed 140 pounds. "Okay, you guys, who wants to help me with the materials we will need for this experiment? I have cones, stopwatches, and a trundle wheel for measuring distance."

With the class gathered in the parking lot, Mr. Morrison assigned 2 students to push behind the truck, 1 student to drive, 1 safety student, 10 students to place cones situated along the route (closer together near the start), 5 timers placed along the route so the cone placer could hear the timer shout out times every 5 seconds, 1 starter to scream "GO" so all timers would start simultaneously, and 4 students to measure distance between the cones. Vicente and Marsha were paired up to be the truck pushers. Phillip was the safety student, and Stevie Camacho got to steer the truck. The rest of the class found their positions, and Mr. Morrison went over the procedures and safety issues with Stevie and Phillip.

With the truck at the starting line, Vicente and Marsha put their bathroom scales on the back door, which was perpendicular to the ground. Mr. Morrison remembered to place a folded up towel under each bathroom scale to avoid any paint scratching. He moved away and with a nod to no one in particular said, "Let the games begin."

Benny yelled "Gooooooooo!" at the top of his lungs, and the timers hit their start buttons. With all the strength they could muster, Vicente and Marsha began pushing the bathroom scales. At first, it took them tremendous force, indicated by the number of pounds on the scales, to start the truck moving. By the time 10 seconds had transpired, they were starting to accelerate, and the force required to push was decreasing. At the sixth cone, Vicente and Marsha realized that they only needed about 20 pounds of force to keep the truck moving at a constant speed, and by the end, they were not able to keep even that amount of force to keep the car moving.

Stevie stopped the car, and he and Phillip got out to celebrate the accomplishment with five high handslaps all around. "Way to go, Vicente, good job,

Marsha," said Mr. Morrison. "Now let's measure the distance to each cone from the starting point to get the data we need to figure out the mass of this little truck here."

Back in the classroom, students worked in small groups to calculate the velocity with respect to displacement and time, and to construct an acceleration versus time graph from the truck data to find the relationship between the shape of velocity versus time and the acceleration versus time graph. Vicente's group was the first to share with the class that the shape for the displacement time graph was parabolic (U-shaped). Mr. Morrison also asked them to calculate the slope of the displacement versus time graphs and the slope of the velocity versus time graphs. Because almost all of the students in this class had taken geometry, and because they knew how to work as teams, they could do the calculations and show their work.

Ultimately, the class was able to come up with a number for the mass of the truck, once Mr. Morrison reintroduced Newton's Second Law, which asserts that an object will only accelerate if there is a net or unbalanced force acting upon it. In this manner, each group of students calculated the mass of the truck using net applied force and average acceleration. Interestingly, the students' mass calculation differed from the mass stated in the owner's manual, so Mr. Morrison asked the class to speculate as to why there was a difference. "That's too easy, Mr. Morrison," Vicente beamed, "in the book, they using balanced mass, but we using net force to get our mass number."

"Yeah, that's easy," said a chorus of students.

In the ensuing week, groups of students wrote up the truck pushing force experiment and sent it off to several high schools in their state for students at those sites to try out as well. With each package they sent, they prepared questions they still had about the experiment, and asked students to give their perspectives on how the experiment worked.

SCIENCE AND ENGLISH LANGUAGE LEARNING

Science classes in secondary school may well be the optimal settings for language acquisition if the classes are hands-on, inquiry-based, and experimental. As we witnessed in Mr. Morrison's class, Vicente and other English learners were successful in learning complex physics concepts by participating in activity after activity in which the requirements for talking, writing, trying out, and being physicists supported their language development as well.

Mr. Morrison's approach to science differs from the more traditional way of teaching science, which emphasizes rote learning of specific scientific facts and the idea that scientists must conduct experiments according to a narrowly conceived, logic-based scientific method. This class is aligned with a broader approach to scientific inquiry, based on the national science standards (National Research Council, 1996), which advocates (1) diversity in the ways scientists inquire about and study the natural world and propose evidence-based explanations derived from their work; (2) observation, problem posing, reference to written and other source material to determine what is already known, problem solving, planning experiments, and predicting and communicating outcomes; and (3) a reduction in the number of concepts that must be taught so that students can develop a deeper understanding of and create stronger identities with how science works.

The broader approach to scientific inquiry that guided Mr. Morrison's physics class provided the English learners in his classes with many of the practices that we know promote English language acquisition for adolescent immigrants such as Vicente and Phillip, who may still be learning English while they are learning academic content. In the following sections, we show how the commitments in practice correspond well to the kinds of practices Mr. Morrison used to make physics challenging, interesting, and supportive of language and literacy development for English learners.

PARTICIPATION AND LEARNING SCIENCE

Mr. Morrison knew from experience and his reading that involving English learners as active participants in the process of scientific inquiry and experimentation meant that he had to rely on hands-on activities that required students to use oral and written language to follow procedures, collect and analyze data, and present findings in a variety of ways. In the beginning of the school year, he had students use talking chips to ensure that every student contributed. He also tried out different grouping structures, such as think-pair-share (Lyman, 1987) and numbered heads together (Kagan, 1989). In this latter structure, each student was assigned a number 1, 2, or 3 as they worked on a problem set. When the problem was completed, he asked all, say, the 2s to raise their hands, and then called on one of these to explain their group's results. In this manner, he encouraged group members to participate actively in the work and to make sure that everyone in the group understood how to communicate the results.

Vicente and the other English learners also were able to participate actively because he set up each set of activities so that students used a wide range of abilities to get through them. In other words, each set of activities involved reading, writing, discussion, calculation, artwork, and oral reporting. This was part of his multiple-abilities approach to learning (Cohen & Lotan, 2004). This approach aims to maximize active participation in heterogeneous classrooms by paying attention to status inequities and designing group work so that, in this case, English speakers, students with high science literacy and mathematics abilities, do not dominate discussion and presentations. Accordingly, Vicente, who struggled with literacy, but was highly capable mathematically, was viewed by his team members as an important resource in problem posing and problem solving. Likewise, Phillip, who read English fluently, but struggled in oral presentations, was provided with lots of support from his team members to prepare for the oral reports.

WORKING TOGETHER AS A COMMUNITY OF LEARNERS

One of Mr. Morrison's favorite phrases was "We are family." He often played and sang along with the song by Sister Sledge with the same message. "Together we learn, alone we don't" was another apothegm he chanted as students were huddled over an experiment. He often reminded students that Einstein and Newton did not come up with their best ideas alone. When a student said something like, "I figured it out," he reminded the class of the expression "There's no 'I' in 'team'."

One of the key components in Mr. Morrison's rule about HELP was that learning physics requires less time lecturing and more time [S − L] working in small groups focused on scientific inquiry and experimental projects with real materials. In the above vignette, students did experiments with Stomper Cars, speeding vehicles, and Mr. Morrison's Ford Explorer. Whole class lectures were limited to previews and reviews of procedures and key vocabulary, and these rarely lasted more than 10 minutes.

Three times a year, Mr. Morrison assigned substantial readings about physicists' lives and how they came up with their ideas. For these readings, Mr. Morrison divided the chapters into jigsaw parts so that team members who read them thoroughly could then share what they learned with their team members (Aronson, Blaney, Stephan, Sikes, & Snapp, 1978). These readings served two main purposes: (1) the integration of biographies into the science class and (2) community building. Mr. Morrison wanted the students to learn about the people behind the ideas that they were studying, and how the people had worked in groups and with other scientists to make their discoveries.

Helping students to see the value of working together went hand in hand with Mr. Morrison's belief that part of learning science was acting in ways that are recognized as essential for becoming a scientist.

LANGUAGE IN SCIENTIFIC LEARNING

One of the most obvious ways that science involves language learning is all of the specialized vocabulary and the particular ways that science defines concepts and expressed actions. Like mathematics and other content areas, science register can be difficult to acquire for all students, but it may be especially challenging to immigrant English learners (Lemke, 1990; Schleppegrell, 2002, 2004; Veel, 1997).

In the activities that Mr. Morrison used to help students understand acceleration, displacement, force, mass, and velocity, he also taught students how to incorporate vocabulary into their group, always insisting that students "try on" new words to see how they fit. He pointed out distinct ways of recognizing and developing definitions commonly used in physics. For example, with acceleration, students could say that it is "how fast the velocity changes" or they could think of it as "the change in velocity divided by the change in time."

Whenever possible, Mr. Morrison tried to provide contextual support for the new concepts and expressions the class would be studying. He did this in several ways:

- Clearly pronouncing speech.
- Using realia (real objects) while showing and telling.
- Using hands, facial expressions, and body movement to accompany descriptions and explanations.
- Pointing to key words, expressions, and ideas while describing and explaining.
- Using different colors to highlight important ideas in text.
- Allowing additional wait time after asking challenging questions.

Moreover, as we saw in the above vignette, Mr. Morrison set up his class so that students constantly *negotiated for meaning* within small groups. Having students of different language and academic abilities exchange information requires them to negotiate for meaning; that is, to clarify ideas, to confirm or disconfirm understanding, to restate ideas, and to use precise language in ways that are aligned with scientific language uses. And, because students always worked with realia and other written support (graphs, artwork, formulae), they had multiple sources of language and context to refer to in their negotiations and discussions. Negotiations for meaning are important from a sociocultural perspective because they enable students to try out and appropriate different ways of expressing meaning through language. As students negotiate, they develop proficiency in language, and at the same time, appropriate the particular register needed for meaningful interaction (see Block, 2003).

THINKING, TALKING, AND EXPERIMENTING LIKE SCIENTISTS

By the time the students in Mr. Morrison's class went out to the parking lot to figure out the mass of his sports utility vehicle, they were already thinking, talking, and inquiring like scientists. They still had to study intensely to appropriate the vocabulary and procedures needed to pose and solve problems involving mass, acceleration, and velocity, but they were "talking science" (Lemke, 1990) and incorporating the physics register Mr. Morrison was constantly using and promoting. The students in Vicente's class not only imagined science communities of practice, but also engaged in them as they moved from problem sets, mini-car experiments, and speeding vehicles to an actual experiment outside the classroom. Every time they plotted and analyzed data, they were expected to use the appropriate register in explaining and justifying their results.

Part of their identity formation as scientists was aided by the use of science equipment and lab room clothing. The young men and women of Mr. Morrison's class enjoyed wearing safety glasses, gloves, and white lab coats. They were careful with the equipment and always put items back in their designated place within the classroom. Mr. Morrison frequently talked with his classes about equipment etiquette and responsible behavior within the science community.

All of these efforts—using physics vocabulary, talking physics, using physics equipment, working in science teams, wearing lab clothing, paying attention to equipment—provided the English learners in Mr. Morrison's class with support for their membership in science communities.

FERRIS HIGH STUDENTS ARE NOT SPEEDING!:
A SCHOOL-COMMUNITY PROJECT

Stevie and Vicente had an idea about how to show the administration whether Ferris High students were indeed exceeding the speed limit around the school when they left campus during lunchtime. The principal wanted to close the campus during lunchtime because he had received several complaints that some of the students had been racing each other and otherwise speeding once they got on the main road to the parking lot entrance of the school. The speed limit was 25 miles an hour.

Stevie and Vicente suggested to Mr. Morrison that they conduct a velocity study over a 2-week period. They needed one more person to help with the experiment. Mr. Morrison approved of the study and recommended that they invite Marsha because she was very precise in her work. Once Marsha agreed, the three of them began by measuring and marking the position $x = 0$ and $x = 100$ meters on the street where the alleged speeding occurred. They measured the 100-meter distance far enough from the school exit so that vehicles would have a chance to maintain a constant velocity. Stevie was the starter and Vicente, the timer. Marsha recorded the time for each vehicle they studied. They decided to choose every fifth vehicle that came out of the parking lot, and they recorded the time for five vehicles on Monday, Wednesday, and Friday for 2 weeks, for a total of 30 velocity times. Once they collected all of the data, they calculated the mean velocity of all the vehicles over 6 days, as well as the mean velocity of the five vehicles for each day they collected data.

Marsha double-checked the calculations, and sure enough, they showed that the average velocity of vehicles coming out of the Ferris High parking lot and onto the main road was 24 miles per hour! On one day, a Friday, they found that the mean velocity was 27 miles per hour, and that was because one car was speeding. Marsha, Stevie, and Vicente shared the experiment and results with the class, and together they decided to write a letter to the principal asking him not to close the campus at lunchtime based on the research findings that Ferris students were not speeding as they were leaving campus during lunchtime.

This use of physics principles to solve a social problem provided a real context for Vicente, Stevie, and Marsha to try on their identities as scientists, and it created a genuine context for authentic language interaction and science register use. When they shared their findings with the class, everyone gave them a round of applause. It was Phillip who thought of the most encouraging kudos: "You guys show that when we are good in science, we have power to tell people that Ferris students aren't bad."

NATIVE LANGUAGE USES IN SCIENCE

Mr. Morrison was not bilingual, but he fostered the use of the native language during small group work, especially for clarification and confirmation checks. Interestingly, in this class, Vicente and the other Spanish-dominant English learners rarely relied on Spanish during small group work. Many of the bilingual Chicano students used Spanish expressions and words, switching from English to Spanish, during small group work, but the main part of their discussions were conducted in English. This is mainly because these students received the lion's share of their formal education in English.

Being able to switch back and forth from English to Spanish is a type of bilingualism that is common among communities in which children grow up hearing and speaking two languages (Zentella, 1997). Students like Vicente, who are not members of the Chicano bilingual community, tend not to switch from one language to the other within sentences. Vicente may eventually appropriate bilingual language switching abilities if he identifies with and participates in Chicano-oriented communities of practice.

One of the ways that Vicente and other Spanish–English bilingual students used their knowledge of Spanish for learning science was by looking for cognates between Spanish and English. Many of the vocabulary words in science have Latin roots, which means that students who know Latin-based languages, such as Spanish, French, and Portuguese, can use this knowledge to help them acquire new vocabulary. In the above unit alone, there were many cognates that made learning new vocabulary easier for Vicente, Stevie, and other bilingual students. For example, in Spanish, velocity is *velocidad* and acceleration is *aceleración*. For Phillip, who also was fluent in French, these two English words also had cognates in French. Mr. Morrison encouraged students to look for cognates as a learning strategy, and he had students share their findings with the entire class to celebrate their bilingualism.

Summary

In this chapter, we have tried to show that English learners can participate in and benefit from science classes that are inquiry-based and hands-on. We included a physics class because it does not matter how complex the scientific concepts are. What matters are the commitments in practice. Mr. Morrison's class employed the commitments in practice in the following ways:

- He aligned his class with a broader approach to scientific inquiry so that students could develop a deeper understanding of and create stronger identities with how science works.

- He relied on hands-on activities that required students to use oral and written language to follow procedures, collect and analyze data, and present findings in a variety of ways, thus using a multiple-abilities approach to learning.

- He maximized heterogeneous groupings by paying attention to status inequities and designing group work so that students with high science literacy and mathematics abilities did not dominate discussion and presentations.

- In addition to common approaches to scaffolding content, such as use of realia, paraverbal support, clearly pronounced speech, highlighting key words (in context), and wait time, he set up his class so that students constantly negotiated for meaning within small groups, giving them the opportunity to clarify ideas, confirm or disconfirm understanding, restate ideas, and use increasingly precise language in ways that are aligned with scientific language uses. Students had multiple sources of language and context to refer to in their negotiations and discussions.

- Mr. Morrison created a scientific community of practice in his classroom by allowing students to walk the walk and talk the talk of science. They wore lab coats and safety glasses, and they practiced the register of science as they conducted experiments both literally and linguistically, trying out new words and appropriating scientific discourses even as they became scientists.

- Students connected to wider contexts when they used their growing knowledge of physics to conduct experiments such as the one Vicente, Stevie, and Marsha undertook to study the speed of cars leaving campus for lunch. A result of the experiment was that the students were able to use physics principles to solve a social problem, allowing them to try on their identities as scientists in a genuine context.

If the classroom and curriculum are organized to be inclusive, participatory, inquiry-oriented, and connected to wider contexts, English learners will not only achieve academically, but also develop their language.

Activities

1. Discuss how you define "negotiate for meaning" and write a short vignette in which two to three students negotiate the meaning of some scientific term or expression that is giving at least one of them some trouble understanding.

2. Suppose you were teaching a ninth grade earth science unit on craters and how they were formed. Half of the students in your class are intermediate English learners, most of whom are at grade level in math and science. You begin by introducing footprints left in the sand and having students hypothesize based on the various depths of the footprints how to measure force and displacement. Design a lesson plan in which you include vocabulary and science register development, small group work, and opportunities for students to use oral and written language as they progress in the lesson. Explain how you will segue into the study of the formation of moon craters.

3. Interview a scientist (biologist, earth scientist, physicist, chemist, astrologist, etc.) to find out about the community of practice in which the scientist works. Ask about inquiry, problem posing, problem solving, the role of literacy in science, and connections of science to technology and the real world. Ask the scientist to comment about what makes high school science ideal for English learners. Compare what you learn from the interview to how Mr. Morrison prepares his students for participating in science communities of practice.

4. Interview several English learners in a science class. Find out what kinds of schooling experiences they had in their primary language. What can you conclude about the role of formal schooling experiences for doing well in science? Ask them to explain what about science learning is easy and difficult and why it is that way for them. What can you conclude from their explanations?

References

Anstrom, K. (1998). *Preparing secondary education teachers to work with English language learners: Science.* Washington, DC: National Clearinghouse for Bilingual Education.

Aronson, E., Blaney, N., Stephan, D., Sikes, J., & Snapp, M. (1978). *The jigsaw classroom.* Beverly Hills, CA: Sage Publications.

Block, D. (2003). *The social turn in second language acquisition.* Edinburgh, England: Edinburgh University Press.

Cohen, E., & Lotan, R. (2004). Equity in heterogeneous classrooms. In J. Banks & C. McGee Banks (Eds.), *Handbook of research on multicultural education* (pp. 736–752). San Francisco, CA: Jossey-Bass.

Kagan, S. (1989). *Cooperative learning resources for teachers*. San Juan Capistrano, CA: Resources for Teachers.

Lemke, J. (1990). *Talking science: Language, learning and values*. Norwood, NJ: Ablex.

Lyman, F. (1987). Think-pair-share: An expanding teaching technique. *MAA-CIE Cooperative News, 1*(1), 1–2.

National Research Council. (1996). *National science education standards*. Washington, DC: National Academy Press.

Schleppegrell, M. J. (2002). Challenges of the science register for ESL students: Errors and meaning making. In M. J. Schleppegrell & M. C. Colombi (Eds.), *Developing advanced literacy in first and second languages: Meaning with power* (pp. 119–142). Mahwah, NJ: Lawrence Erlbaum.

Schleppegrell, M. J. (2004). *The language of schooling: A functional linguistics perspective*. Mahwah, NJ: Lawrence Erlbaum.

Veel, R. (1997). Learning how to mean—scientifically speaking: Apprenticeship into scientific discourse in the secondary school. In F. Christie & J. R. Martin (Eds.), *Genre and institutions: Social processes in the workplace and school* (pp. 161–195). London: Cassell Publishers.

Zentella, C. (1997). *Growing up bilingual*. Oxford, England: Blackwell Publisher.

8 Assessment with Adolescent English Learners

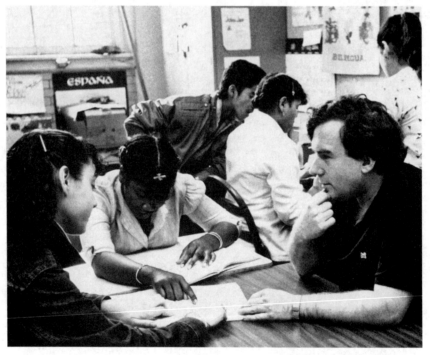

Laimute Druskis/PH College

OVERVIEW

In this chapter, we discuss different forms of assessments, and the role of assessment in instruction of secondary English learners. There are two main issues to consider with assessment: (1) using assessment appropriately to guide learning, and (2) identifying and reclassifying English language services. All secondary schools are required to identify students whose primary language is not English and to evaluate the level of their English proficiency to determine whether they are eligible for English language support services. We begin with assessment to guide instruction and follow this with a discussion on placement and evaluation of English proficiency for identification and reclassification of English learners and the types of tests used to make these important decisions.

ASSESSMENT THAT ASSISTS LEARNING

Imagine an ice skater trying to master her axle jump. Her coach stands by her on the ice as she makes attempt after attempt to land her jump. Imagine the skater approaches the jump, bends her knees, throws her body into the air, then falls hard on the ice. She looks at her coach, and he says, "That's about a D." She stands up, makes her approach again, bends her knees, and throws her body into another spin in the air. She doesn't fall this time, but lands on two feet. "Better," her coach says. "About a C-plus." She stands up, and continues to attempt her jump, sometimes falling, sometimes not, but never quite landing a proper axle.

Now imagine our same skater. She makes her first jump, and her coach says, "You fell because you didn't lift your knee up. Remember, lift that leg straight up." She tries again, this time lifting up her knee. She doesn't fall, but lands on two feet. "Okay, better," the coach says. "See, when you lift your knee up, you get the height to make the rotation. Now try it again. Don't forget to lift that knee up, but this time also remember to bring your arms in directly to your chest as you take off. That will give you more rotation." She tries it again and again. Each time the coach gives her an assessment of specific body positioning, and more instruction as to how to improve her jump through immediate, individualized feedback.

Our skater will make faster progress with the latter kind of assessment. She will make even more if the coach has a strong understanding of her learning dispositions and background. Does the skater know her edges? Is she afraid of falling? Can she land in a back spin? Even more specific, what other jumps has she mastered? How does she feel about skating? How is she feeling that day? The good coach will know all of this and more when assessing his skater, and will take all of these elements into account when he gives her feedback. Specific feedback will help her learn her axle much faster than a simple grade will.

Assessment is closely tied to instruction. It is a partnership, one relying on the other in every learning event. We feel that recent laws and the move toward high-stakes testing has distanced assessment from instruction to the detriment of all learners, but especially to English learners. All learners need specific assessment tied to learning events, individualized feedback that helps them grow. Such feedback is as much a part of the process of learning as it is a part of learning products.

Informal and Formal Assessment.

There are two basic kinds of assessment: informal, instructional forms of assessments and formal district, state, and federal assessments (O'Malley & Pierce, 1996). Both kinds of assessments make the claim that students' skills and abilities are analyzed, compared, quantified, scored, or otherwise appropriately expressed through different means.

Our skater and her coach were engaged in a learning event in which assessment was instruction-based and informal. Imagine that our skater goes on to the national USFSA organization for testing. These tests are considered objective and unbiased, a formal form of assessment. Judges, who are often active coaches themselves, sit on a panel and watch as our skater displays her different skating skills. They give her scores and decide whether she should pass her skating test. Insiders to the skating world know that these "objective" tests are often political, determined by club and coach-to-coach affiliations. But let's just say for the point of demonstration that these tests are objective. What kind of information does our skater get? On the day of the test she is told that she either passes or doesn't pass each individual skill. If she lands her axle but doesn't pass that skill, she is not given any information as to why she didn't pass. Were her arms up on the landing? Did she take off from the wrong edge? Why didn't she pass it? By the same token, if she passes, she doesn't know why she passed. What did she do right? She learns that, in this particular place and time, according to this panel of judges, her axle either passed or didn't pass, in comparison with other skaters within the USFSA organization.

Assuming the assessment of the one or two jumps she does on that one given test situation is accurate, our skater now knows how she compares with other skaters nationally. Or does she? What if she had the stomach flu that day? What if one of her skates wasn't tied properly? What if she was nervous and didn't perform her axle as well as she usually does when she practices? Or what if her nerves caused her to put more force into her takeoff, and she actually lands the jump like she never has in her life. What if she just happened to get it right for the first time in that test event, but doesn't know how or why? Can we still claim that she can "do an axle"? These are issues related to the reliability of formal, standardized assessments.

Our stance is that formal, standardized assessments provide information in a one-time testing event, and this information may be problematic or even inaccurate as in the case of our ice skater. And as in the case of our skater, the objectivity and trustworthiness of such assessments is suspect (Wiggins, 1992; Graves, 2002).

ASSESSMENTS, INSTRUCTION, AND ACCOUNTABILITY

Different kinds of assessments fulfill different purposes for different entities. Informal classroom assessment usually fulfills teachers' needs for instruction-based assessment. Teachers observe ongoing, daily learning activities and interactions so that they can assess progress over time, habits, attitudes, and social interactions around content. This ongoing, daily assessment assists teachers in instructional planning. Teachers may also use more formal assessments that are closely tied to instruction. These assessments might include portfolios, learning inventories, process learning activities, and learning products such as presentations, celebrations, and written reports as indicators of learning. Miscue analysis, rubrics, self-assessments, and others all work together to help assess student learning.

In addition to the repertoire of informal instruction-based assessments that the teacher has at hand, many formal, standards-based assessments are available. Indeed, many are required. Although these assessments can yield useful information regarding student learning, their purpose is driven by a different source: a nationwide call for accountability. District, state, and federal mandates require increasingly specific skills and information to be taught and assessed in the classroom. Instruction is standards-based (rather than needs-based), and teachers must show that the standards have been taught and learned. As a response to this move toward account-ability in teaching, districts and states require the administration of specific assessments, some more useful than others.

Recalling our ice skater at the beginning of the chapter, our view is that the best form of assessment is instruction-based assessments, such as the coach giving the skater specific feedback in the act of skating. However, standards-based curriculum with high-stakes testing require-ments are a reality in today's classrooms. In the following sections, we discuss how both kinds of assessments reside and flourish in each of our content-based classrooms. We begin with a detailed discussion of Mrs. MacPherson's assessment practices in her language arts class.

ASSESSING ENGLISH LEARNERS IN LANGUAGE ARTS: AN EXAMPLE OF ASSESSMENT TO GUIDE LEARNING

Mrs. MacPherson's language arts classroom included many opportu-nities for daily, ongoing assessments. Mrs. MacPherson kept a three-ring binder with dividers for sections for each student in her class. In this binder, Mrs. MacPherson collected all types of formal and infor-mal assessments. In Alex's section of the assessment binder, Mrs. MacPherson had the following items:

1. A copy of a miscue analysis Mrs. MacPherson had conducted at the beginning of the year, along with follow-up mini-miscues that she had conducted during various conferences with Alex. A few sticky notes were pasted to the miscue markings, each with notes Mrs. MacPherson made. One said, "Increasing use of semantic cues for prediction-making" along with the date. At the end of each quarter, Mrs. MacPherson could look back at the miscues and assess Alex's progress over time in reading.

2. A page titled "Alex as a Reader" on which Mrs. MacPherson had written various notes, always with the date. On this page, Mrs. MacPherson wrote all of her observations about Alex as a reader in various reading activities throughout the year. Mrs. MacPherson always walks around her room with a clipboard with sticky notes. She writes observations on her sticky notes during the class period. She transfers these notes to her binder when she gets the chance. Sometimes when Mrs. MacPherson gets busy, she simply puts the sticky notes on the page, making sure to date them. At the end of the quarter, Mrs. MacPherson has lots of data from which to assess her students.

3. A page titled, "Alex as a Writer." On this page, Mrs. MacPherson includes anecdotes and observations of Alex during various writing activities. As with the previous page, Mrs. MacPherson always dates her entries on this page.

4. Skills and Strategies in Reading. This page is identical to one that Alex keeps in his reading log. This page includes a list of skills and strategies that Alex and Mrs. MacPherson agree that he should work on as he reads independently. Alex keeps notes on his page as Mrs. MacPherson keeps notes on hers. He refers to it when needed in his various reading activities.

5. Skills and Strategies in Writing. Alex keeps an identical page in his writing folder. On this page Alex and Mrs. MacPherson take notes from conferences or guided writing groups about specific skills Alex is working on in his writing.

6. A copy of all formal district and state assessments.

Examples of numbers 2 through 6 can be found in Table 8.1. At the beginning of the year much of the assessment focuses on the identity and habits of the reader/writer. As the year goes on, more focus will be placed on strong craft and deeper meaning, including the all-important place of conventions (grammar, spelling, vocabulary, etc.) in powerful writing.

Mrs. MacPherson sometimes includes copies of work samples from Alex to illustrate his growing skills in reading and writing, but she limits these because of space. Work samples are collected and stored in other files, and each of her students keeps portfolios (discussed below), so many of the samples are housed there. Mrs. MacPherson is very careful to date every document and note. If she gets busy during the semester and doesn't have time to log ongoing assessments in her binder pages, she can reflect on all of her sticky notes and such at the end of the semester when she is figuring final grades. That's not to say that Mrs. MacPherson ignores this information until grading time. Her thoughts and observations are active aspects of her instructional planning.

As Mrs. MacPherson observes Alex in his interactions around literacy, she also keeps tabs of how Alex is progressing in terms of state and district standards. At the front of her binder, Mrs. MacPherson has a spreadsheet with each student's name in the rows, and each of the standards in the columns. Periodically during the semester, Mrs. MacPherson uses this spreadsheet to date when specific standards have been introduced, practiced, and mastered. The spreadsheet helps Mrs. MacPherson be aware of district and state guidelines as she plans

Table 8.1
Teacher Notes for Assessing Alex as a Reader and Writer

ALEX AS A READER

Date	Notes
9/7	Alex likes basketball and karate. Two brothers, one older, one younger. Been in U.S. two years. Semi-literate in Native Laotian.
9/15	Conducted reading interest inventory. Doesn't like to read, and only reads school-related books.
9/23	Conducted miscue analysis. Alex overrelies on phonics as a language cue. Must focus on more meaning-making strategies.
9/30	Guided reading group with Tony, Rebecca, and Marisol. Began *A Single Shard* by Linda Sue Park. Character map and discussion on building schema. Group will read as lit. circle.
10/5	Lit. circle meeting. Alex engaging in story. Commented, "Tree-Ear is both young and old sometimes." Good insight. Needs. vocab. support. Will conf. to start log.
10/7	Conference and mini-miscue. More evidence of meaning-making strategies (see markings). Started vocab. log.
10/14	Lit. circle. Alex noted the simple voice of the story, saying he'd like to try it in his writing piece (fiction on gangs). Read passage from book to illustrate. (Note: May like *An Island Like You*—he reminds me of Arturo.)

ALEX AS A WRITER

Date	Notes
9/6	Started writer's notebook. Struggles with vocab. Suggested he use placeholders when drafting. Can use Laotian, but he's not comfortable writing it.
9/16	Started a story about a boy in a gang. Seems very engaged. Using placeholders to draft.
9/23	Has a good rough draft. Seems reluctant to revise—wants to go directly to editing. Eager to learn English.
10/3	Began writing poetry today, based on Gary Soto's *Neighborhood Odes*. He loves it.
10/14	Reading *A Single Shard*. Decided to go back and craft gang story a little more. Good progress on revision skills.
11/1	Improvement on verb tenses and vocab. Conference on ways to work with words in log. Will add class word wall.
11/22	Eager to share poem in read around. Got to class early to set up. Commented on humor in Sergei's piece.

SKILLS AND STRATEGIES IN READING—ALEX

Date	Notes
9/15	Begin exploring interests in reading. Read 15–30 mins. daily at home.
9/23	Use schema to predict meaning. Use what you know to figure out what you don't know.
9/30	Use semantic maps (character maps, story boards, etc.) in reading log to help with comprehension.
10/7	Continue to use meaning clues to predict and confirm. Start vocab. log.
10/14	Great job making connections! Continue to connect your reading to your writing.

SKILLS AND STRATEGIES IN WRITING—ALEX

Date	Notes
9/6	Use placeholders when you don't know a word. You can come back to it when you revise and edit.
9/23	Revise and craft before you edit. Use revision and editing lists. Peer conference with a buddy.
10/3	Great poetry! When editing story, focus on proper verb tense. Use reference guides I gave you.
10/14	Continue to craft as you write and revise. Use reading as a guide to writing craft.
10/26	Think about word choice in writing. Use strong verbs. Try the thesaurus for ideas, add new words to vocab. log.

Table 8.2

Classroom Activities and Corresponding Assessments

Activity	Assessments
Individual conferences	• Use of language cues and meaning-making strategies in reading • Skills and conventions in writing • Topics and genre of interest (i.e., is the student progressing in multiple genres and topics) • Ability to craft, revise, and edit writing • Growth of student as reader/writer
Guided literacy groups	• Skills, strategies, and conventions • Ability to work in small groups
Literature circles	• Comprehension • Ability to make inferences • Ability to make connections • Social interactions around books
Minilessons	• Skills, strategies, and conventions • Follow up to see if student is applying new concepts in other literacy activities
Shared reading/writing	• Knowledge of syntactic structures • Skills, strategies, and conventions
Independent writing	• Identity as writer • Growth as writer • Ability to use writing process
Independent reading	• Identity as reader • Growth as reader • Skills, strategies, and conventions
Read around discussions	• Knowledge of writing craft • Making connections • Growth of class community
Class participation	• Identifying with class community • Participating academically and socially • Contribution to class community

instruction. Student needs drive her curriculum, but Mrs. MacPherson is able to cover the standards because she knows them and how each student is progressing toward them. State and district standards are usually general enough that a curriculum can be needs-based and still meet standards.

Mrs. MacPherson also keeps an index of students' names and class dates. Every day she checks off the names of students with whom she conferences or meets in small group meetings. She also checks the names of students for whom she has made notes or observations. Each morning Mrs. MacPherson checks this index so that she can make sure that every student is being observed and assessed on an ongoing basis. With a load of 150 students each day, it is paramount that Mrs. MacPherson take notes and have an organized system for ongoing assessments.

Table 8.2 shows each literacy activity and the kinds of assessments that can result from them.

At the end of each grading period, Mrs. MacPherson has a binder full of authentic assessments as well as formal district and state assessments from which to evaluate the progress of her students. Oftentimes she finds that formal assessments don't have the complete picture, including the all-important progress over time. Her ongoing informal assessments fill the gap, and she has plenty of evidence of progress (or lack of adequate progress) to show to parents and administrators. More important, these ongoing assessments have provided guidance for instructional planning.

ASSESSING ENGLISH LEARNERS IN OTHER CONTENT AREAS

By looking closely at Mrs. MacPherson's assessment structures, we can glean some important ideas for assessment in other academic content areas. Here are some principles and valuable recommendations to consider when working with English learners and immigrant students:

1. Daily, ongoing assessment is vital for instructional planning as well as for authentic measures of student growth. You should collect some kind of assessment data each day. You can keep a journal, make notes, have students place their daily work in personal folders, and ask students to self-assess their understanding. Talk with your students individually about their progress.

2. It is helpful to have an organized system for collecting assessment data. Each semester organize a filing system in which you build a portfolio for each of your students (see below for a discussion of

portfolios). For English learners, you should include a language proficiency profile that includes language strengths and areas of need. Be sure to collect samples of reading and writing abilities, especially samples that provide evidence of using academic register literacy. You can also include tape recordings of oral reports, journal entries, PowerPoint presentations, artwork, letters, poems, rap music, brainstorms, graphic organizers, illustrations, and observation notes.

3. Teachers can use both informal and formal assessments to guide instruction. Under NCLB, students in secondary school have to take formal assessments. Prepare your students for these tests, but also talk with them about the informal assessments you use and how these assessments help guide your teaching (Cushman, 2000; Chamot & O'Malley, 1994). Use a variety of ways to assess mastery and improvement, not just multiple-choice tests. See number 2 above for examples.

4. Progress toward district and state standards can be reflected in both informal and formal assessments. You can show students how well they are doing on district and state standards through a variety of means. You can prepare English learners for formal tests by having students understand the ways you assess them informally.

5. Specific, timely feedback is necessary for student growth. For assessment to be effective for learning, students need to have feedback on what they are doing well and what they need to improve. This is especially important for school districts that use benchmark standards throughout the school year to check for learning progress. In addition to you providing timely feedback from assessments, you can and should teach English learners to continually ask questions of their peers about how well they understand and are able to perform academic activities. Students can learn assessment questions, such as "What is the problem asking us? What is another way to ask this question? What are the main parts of this problem?" These questions help students monitor their own learning (Boaler, 2006). English learners are successful when they understand what being successful academically means (Chamot & O'Malley, 1994; Haley & Austin, 2004).

6. Grades should come from a plethora of assessment data, not from a list of final products. To honor process learning, process learning is what should be addressed. Especially with English learners who are still struggling with English, the grades you give should reflect

the language proficiency standards used in your state and district (Teachers of English to Speakers of Other Languages, [TESOL], 1997). Using rubric-based performance assessment, for example, provides a way for English learners to show learning, and for you to grade that learning based on predetermined indicators of their performance (Haley & Austin, 2004). Rubrics are progress indicators presented in the form of assessment scales used to evaluate student performance in literacy and academic content areas. For more ideas on using rubric-based assessments, progress indicators, and grading English learners, see Haley and Austin (2004), *The help! kit* (Wrigley, 2001), and the *ESL Standards for Pre-K–12 Students* (TESOL, 1997).

WHY MULTIPLE ASSESSMENTS ARE NEEDED FOR ENGLISH LEARNERS

When schools rely on single measures to assess language proficiency and academic achievement, the results almost always work against efforts to ensure success among English learners. Single measures place English learners at risk of failing in all-English classrooms. For example, in Arizona, which relies on a single language proficiency measure to assess whether English learners have reached "reasonable fluency" in English, students who score at a certain level on the proficiency test are no longer eligible to receive English language support for the rest of their high school experience. With multiple assessments of their English abilities, teachers can make much better decisions about whether English learners are ready for all-English classrooms without additional support. Multiple assessments for language proficiency also provide teachers with content-sensitive information about how well students use language within different aspects of the curriculum. This information is useful for guiding instruction to better meet their language needs (Gottlieb, 1999).

Likewise, when schools use one formal assessment to determine academic achievement, English learners are placed at a disadvantage because formal assessments of content knowledge is language based. Single formal assessments give English learners one shot at demonstrating achievement; multiple assessments enable teachers to diagnose strengths and weaknesses and adjust teaching accordingly. This is not to say that English learners do not need to take formal assessments. Rather, the point is that multiple assessments, formal and informal, provide a wider view of English learners' achievement in school.

ELLs are particularly vulnerable to high-stakes decisions based on test results; tests are used to make decisions regarding high school graduation, grade promotion, and the placement of ELLs into tracked programs. (Menken, 2000, p. 3)

In high school, in particular, once English learners are placed into tracked programs or are retained, the probability of them dropping out of high school goes up considerably (Harklau, 1994; Rumberger, 2004). Using multiple assessments is one of the ways that teachers can use to mitigate against this costly and shameful result.

SETTING UP AN ASSESSMENT SYSTEM

To set up a system of assessment in other content areas, you can use the same concept Mrs. MacPherson used. The first step is to create a filing system or three-ring binder that includes each student's name. You will need to decide which concepts and learning attributes are most important in the specific content area. You will need to conduct daily, ongoing observations and take notes on what students are doing and how well they seem to be doing. Whenever possible, you should include specific assessment data, and you should focus on growth over time (rather than some arbitrary level). For example, in social studies, the teacher may focus on specific historical concepts for each unit (including, of course, district and state standards). In addition, the teacher will want to include ongoing assessments on each student as a learner of history. Is the student able to conduct research and glean information from multiple sources? Can the student critically examine resources for bias? Can the student contextualize historical events in each time period? Does the student understand cause and effect? Learner attributes such as ability to work in a group and contribute to the community of practice are also important assessments to conduct. Evidence of learning can be collected from both informal and formal assessments. Products such as oral and PowerPoint presentations and written reports can reflect learning, but so can group discussions, illustrations, and group projects.

In the math and science classes, teachers can examine student work that asked them to show their calculations and write about what they were thinking in trying to solve the problem. They can ask simple questions, such as "Can the student do the operations? Can the student use specialized vocabulary appropriately?" As in Mrs. MacPherson's language arts classroom, a clipboard and sticky notes can be used to document evidence of learning throughout the day. Teachers can also develop rubrics with performance indicators on a scale from shows little understanding to shows full understanding. In both instances, the goal is to assess what students are learning and to use this information to guide continued instruction.

Learning products are, of course, an additional source of assessment information. This is especially true for products that include the learning process. For example, a project that the student works on over time, and for which the teacher gives ongoing feedback (as opposed to a one-shot performance) can yield more evidence and information about learning than a unit test.

USING PORTFOLIOS WITH ENGLISH LEARNERS

Portfolios are a worthwhile form of assessment for all content areas (French, 1992). The best portfolios include examples of work that reflect growth over time, including not only the best products, but also evidence of learning through process (Haley & Austin, 2004). For example, a portfolio might include parts of projects from the beginning, middle, and end of the semester; some photocopies of pages from a learning log; and an essay by the student reflecting on his progress over the course of the grading period. Oftentimes students decide what to include in the portfolio. In this way, students are put in charge of their own learning.

Every teacher has her unique style, and will have different approaches to assessment. However, we feel it is paramount that teachers draw from multiple sources for assessment, the most important of which is specific and ongoing, centered in authentic learning activities with a focus toward progress over time. Portfolios offer you a means to accomplish this.

ASSESSMENT FOR IDENTIFICATION AND RECLASSIFICATION

In this final section, we discuss assessment procedures used to identify, reclassify, and exit English learners from English language support services.

Entry, Reclassification, and Exit Criteria

In secondary school, getting in and out of English language development (often called English-as-a-second-language) programs is largely determined by tests. In this section, we will examine the kinds of procedures and tests that are commonly used for identifying eligible students, for assessing their language proficiency, for reclassifying them once they are in a program, and finally, for exiting them from the program.

PORTFOLIOS WITH ENGLISH LEARNERS

For more information on using portfolios with English learners, consult the following.

Bibliography

French, R. (1992). Portfolio assessment and LEP students. In *Proceedings of the second National Research Symposium on limited English proficient student issues: Focus on evaluation and measurement,* Vol. 1 (pp. 249–272). Washington, DC: U.S. Department of Education.

Gottlieb, M. (1999). Assessing ESOL adolescents: Balancing accessibility to learn with accountability for learning. In C. Faltis & P. Wolfe (Eds.), *So much to say: Adolescents, bilingualism, and ESL in the secondary school* (pp. 176–204). New York: Teachers College Press.

La Celle-Peterson, W., & Rivera, C. (1994). Is it real for all kids: A framework for equitable assessment policies for English language learners. *Harvard Educational Review 69*(1), 55–75.

O'Malley, M., & Pierce, L. (1996). *Authentic assessment for English language learners: Practical approaches for teachers.* New York: Addison-Wesley.

All of the tests that we present are worthy of some criticism; they can hardly be called authentic assessments of how students use language for communication with a variety of audiences. Nonetheless, it is important to know about them and to use additional means of assessment to make sense of how well students use language for oral and written communication about academic content in your classes.

Determining Program Eligibility

The Lau Remedies of 1974 made the identification of students whose primary language is not English and the evaluation of their English language proficiency mandatory. The first step in determining eligibility for English language and bilingual services is to identify students whose first language is not English. When parents register their child at a school, they are asked to complete a survey which asks four questions:

1. Was your child's first language a language other than English?
2. Is a language other than English spoken in the home?
3. Is the language most often spoken by your child a language other than English?
4. Do you speak a language other than English to your child most of the time?

An answer of "yes" to any of these four questions by parents indicates that the student's primary home language is other than English. Once this has been determined, the next step is to find out the student's level of English proficiency and whether he or she is eligible for bilingual and/or English language support services.

The criteria for entering a special instructional program at the secondary level vary from state to state, but most states determine entry eligibility on the basis of oral and written English proficiency test scores. Unfortunately, most high schools do not administer a home language reading assessment or inquiry about home language reading abilities (O'Malley & Pierce, 1996). Three popular English proficiency tests are the Language Assessment Scales (LAS), the Language Assessment Battery (LAB), and the Stanford English Language Proficient (SELP) test. Individual states have developed their own language proficiency tests. Other tests are the Basic Inventory of Natural Language (BINL), the Bilingual Syntax Measure (BSM), and the Individualized Developmental English Activities (IDEA) Placement Test (Samway & McKeon, 1999). However, these tests were not initially designed for use in high school settings. The SELP test (Harcourt Brace, 2003) is the most recent of language proficiency tests, and it is gaining popularity nationwide. This test assesses listening, speaking, reading, written conventions, and writing abilities using picture cues and language text and has versions for primary, elementary, middle, and high school students. The SELP test claims to be aligned with NCLB standards and local state standards of language proficiency. The most commonly used standardized English reading tests are the Comprehensive Test of Basic Skills (CTBS) and the California Achievement Test (CAT). When available, schools that do assess home language literacy most often choose the following non-English-language standardized reading tests: the Spanish version of LAS, the Spanish version of BSM, and the Spanish version of the SELP.

To get an idea of what oral English proficiency tests propose to measure and how they distinguish levels of proficiency, we will examine two popular tests, the LAS and the SELP test, in greater detail. (For reviews of language proficiency tests mentioned above as well as many others, see Alderson, Krahnke, & Stansfield, 1987; and Samway & McKeon, 1999.)

The Language Assessment Scales

The LAS is an individually administered test that was developed by Edward DeAvila and Sharon Duncan in the late 1970s (McGroarty, 1987). There are two versions: LAS I for grades 2 through 5, and LAS II for grade 6 and up. Both versions measure oral language skills in English and in Spanish based on a student's performance on four linguistic subsystems, which include the sound system, vocabulary, syntax, and pragmatics (the ability to complete certain tasks in the language). Computer-based versions of the LAS are currently available. The sound system is assessed by having students indicate whether minimal pairs of words sound the same or different (30 items) and by having them repeat certain sounds of the language (36 items). Vocabulary is tested by having the student name items pictured in the test (20 items). Syntax is measured through two subscales, oral comprehension and oral production of a story presented on an audiocassette. The assessment of pragmatic ability is optional and consists of 10 questions that draw out the student's ability to use language for describing and narrating without the use of story props.

Students are assigned to one of five proficiency levels on the basis of total correct responses that are converted to weighted scores. Level 1 indicates that the student is non-English proficient (NEP). Level 2 is also non-English proficient with some isolated language abilities. Level 3 students are designated as limited English proficient (LEP), and levels 4 and 5 mean that students are fully English proficient (FEP) and highly articulate, respectively. After reviewing the LAS tests, MacSwan (2000) asserts that "the test is so poorly designed that literally no conclusions regarding a child's linguistic abilities may be drawn" from any particular score.

The Stanford English Language Proficiency Test

The SELP test was developed as a means for schools to identify and place students, to measure outcomes and show progress, to evaluate programs, and to plan instruction (Harcourt Brace, 2003). The test is available in English and Spanish. There are five levels of the SELP test: kindergarten, primary (grades 1–2), elementary (grades 3–5), middle school (grades 6–8), and high school (grades 9–12). The middle school and high school tests are group administered for listening, writing conventions, reading, and extended writing. Speaking tests are individually administered and take approximately 15 minutes per student. The speaking test is scored on a point system from 0 (no fluency) to 2 (good fluency). A score of 1 indicates some spoken fluency. The writing test uses a 4-point scoring system that indicates levels of mastery of writing conventions, spelling, grammatical structure, vocabulary use, length, and intelligibility.

Student scores across listening, speaking, reading, and total writing (written conventions and extended writing) are reported using the proficiency levels of preemergent, emergent, basic, intermediate, and proficient. Individual scores are also available for academic (reading, written conventions, and extended writing), social (listening and speaking), and productive (speaking and extended writing) language performance.

The SELP test also offers teachers and schools two types of English learner profiles that are valuable for guiding instruction. The individual Student Report provides a breakdown and narrative for language proficiency for language (listening, speaking, reading, and writing) and communicative (academic, social, and productive) skills. This report indicates the student's performance level and gives a scaled score for each skill along with a total score that determines the student's proficiency level at the time of the test. The scaled score is important because it determines the weight of the particular skill being measured. The Department of Education in each state sets the weight of each skill area.

The second profile provided through the SELP test is the Class Proficiency Report. This report provides a breakdown of the scores of all English learners in a particular class, divided into proficiency levels. This helps the teacher know where the students are with respect to oral and written language proficiency, and what they need to work on to progress to the next level.

Problems with Language Proficiency Tests

An area of critical concern with the SELP test is that because State Departments of Education can determine the weights of the various skills being measured, they can manipulate how easy or difficult it is for English learners to become reclassified as proficient, and thus, no longer eligible for English language services. Politically, this also means that in states such as Arizona, California, and Massachusetts, which have passed English-only schooling laws, the weighting of skill areas enables State Departments of Education to apply lower weights so that English learners are reclassified as proficient within one year. For example, in Arizona, which operates under the assumption that students can become "reasonably fluent" in English within a year (Arizona Revised Statute § 15–752; Molera, 2001), the State Department of Education has set the weights lower for reading and writing than speaking and listening, with the result that thousands of English learners are being reclassified as proficient and thus, no longer in need of special English language services. These students are at risk of underachieving in all-English classes without continued English language support.

Both of these proficiency tests are also limited because they assume that students will perform in English when called on to do so. Older English learners, especially those with nonparallel schooling experiences, may respond differently to requests to answer questions to which the answers are already known. There are also differences in how English learners from different cultures respond to questions posed by unfamiliar adults. These tests, which are based on performance, do not take the effect of possible cultural differences in response into account. So, for example, if a student chooses not to label certain items or not to create a narrative from a sequence of pictures, the student may be labeled "preemergent or emergent." It may be, however, that the student has chosen not to talk because the test asks for language use that violates the norms of the student's home and community.

Both the LAS and the SELP test assess how well students can respond to and pick out things that the test developers believe to represent language proficiency. Neither test presents language as a whole system, one that cannot be fragmented into isolated sounds, sentence patterns, and recall formats. Our suggestion is that if you have to use any of these tests or ones like them, use them judiciously, and always look for additional, alternative ways of assessing language ability. Also, be sure to inquire about home language abilities, and pay lots of attention to how students use language within the multiple settings of your classroom.

Reclassification and Exit Criteria

Reclassification refers to the practice of regularly assessing English learners to determine continued eligibility for language-related instructional assistance. In English-only programs, such as structured English immersion and English as a second language, as well as in transitional bilingual programs, reclassifying a student as proficient or reasonably fluent means that the student is ready to exit out of the special program. In this manner, exiting and reclassification are not distinguished in a majority of cases (Cardoza, 1986).

Assessing students to determine continued eligibility is usually done once a year, in the final weeks of school. Most school districts assess English oral language proficiency as a part of their exit criteria, and most use the same tests employed for entry eligibility. The cutoff scores used for program exit are usually those recommended by the test publisher in consultation with the State Department of Education. When standardized English tests are used for exit purposes, there is considerable variation across states as to the cutoff percentile score used for discontinuing program eligibility (Ovando, Collier, & Combs, 2003). New York, for example, uses the 40th percentile. Arizona exits English learners from programs when they score at or above the 36th percentile on a standardized English test or when they test as proficient on the SELP test. In Texas, students are exited from the program when they score between the 23rd and the 40th percentile on a standardized English test. Clearly, these exit criteria place many adolescent English learners at risk of not finishing high school.

Many of the better school districts that have bilingual and/or ESL programs rely on other information to determine when to exit a student out of a program. Some districts, for example, make exit decisions for students in bilingual and ESL programs based on the following criteria: (1) teacher evaluation of the student's oral English language proficiency; (2) assessment of English oral language proficiency as measured by state-designated proficiency tests (LAS, BSM, IDEA, BINL, or SELP); (3) assessment of writing ability as measured by teacher-scored writing samples or standardized tests; (4) assessment of English language arts (spelling, punctuation, and reading comprehension); and (5) consultation with parents to ensure that final classification is appropriate. States that do have multiple exit criteria rely primarily on the first three areas of assessment (Samway & McKeon, 1999).

CONCLUSION

Evidence of student learning can be shown through many means, from informal to formal standardized tests. Assessment guides instruction, and so it is vital that teachers have a system through which they can collect, organize, reflect on, and document learning. Teaching is much like conducting research, in which data is collected and warrant made based on evidence. Assessment goes way beyond awarding points for the quality of a project or giving a test. Multiple means of assessment is the cornerstone of good teaching and the academic achievement.

Identifying and reclassifying English learners continues to be problematic because language proficiency tests provide a narrow picture of what students are capable of doing with language. High school teachers must use multiple measures of language proficiency to supplement single language proficiency assessments. When all is said and done, your assessment practices should reflect and support the commitments in practice you adopt in your classroom as well as your dedication to ensuring the academic achievement of English learners and immigrant students.

Summary

Assessment has become increasingly prevalent in secondary school. It ranges from high-stakes to local classroom testing. All secondary teachers need to be aware of the value and pitfalls of various types of assessments used in school to diagnose learning needs, to show progress, to make exit decisions for English learners, and to graduate from high school. Here are some of the key ideas this chapter presents:

- There are multiple ways to assess student performance and progress.
- Teachers should focus on growth of learning over time.
- Content area standards provide information on the kinds of abilities and knowledge students should achieve.
- Teachers can compose rubrics for specific kinds of abilities and knowledge and tie these to standards.
- Portfolios offer teachers a wide range of sources from which to assess student performance and progress.
- All secondary schools are required to determine eligibility for English language support services for English learners.
- In addition to packaged English language proficiency tests, teachers should use additional information to ensure English learners are ready to succeed in all-English classrooms.

At the secondary level, assessment can be devastating to English learners, especially in states that require passing an exam to graduate. It is up to teachers to advocate for English learners to ensure that assessment is used fairly and for purposes of indicating learning needs and learning gains.

Activities

1. Organize into content area groups, and for each of the content area chapters and content areas represented in your class, look for multiple ways to informally assess how well students are learning and using language to learn. Suggest additional ways of assessing based on suggested strategies presented in this chapter.

2. What kinds of evidence for learning and improvement would you place in students' portfolios? What kinds of evidence would you have your students place in their portfolios? Explain how the portfolio contents would provide evidence for spoken and written language development and academic content knowledge growth.

3. Become familiar with the language proficiency tests used in your secondary school. Does your school assess literacy in the student's home language? Why is it important to know about the student's prior literacy experiences and abilities? How do the language assessment proficiency scores relate to the English language proficiency standards used in your school? How and how often are students' individual scores reported to teachers?

4. Develop a set of rubrics for English learners to assess their own learning of particular content in your classroom. Develop a set of rubrics to assess English learners' reading and writing abilities within your academic content area.

5. Observe your English learners in various activity settings, and write notes on how they are participating, the kind of language they are using, and what they are learning. How does this kind of assessment add to other forms of informal assessment that you use in class?

References

Alderson, C. J., Krahnke, K. J., & Stansfield, C. W. (Eds.). (1987). *Reviews of English language proficiency tests*. Washington, DC: TESOL.

Boaler, J. (2006). Urban success: A multidimensional mathematics approach with equitable outcomes. *Phi Delta Kappan, 87*(5), 364–369.

Cardoza, D. (1986). The identification and reclassification of limited English proficient students: A study of entry and exit classification procedures. *NABE Journal, 11*(1), 21–45.

Chamot, A., & O'Malley, M. (1994). *The CALLA handbook: Implementing the cognitive academic language learning approach*. Reading, MA: Addison-Wesley.

Cushman, K. (2000). "Everything we do is for a purpose, and we get something out of it": A case study of Landmark High School, New York, NY. *Reinventing high school: Six journeys of change*. Boston, MA: Jobs for the Future.

French, R. (1992). Portfolio assessment and LEP students. In *Proceedings of the second National Research Symposium on limited English proficient student issues: Focus on evaluation and measurement*, Vol. 1 (pp. 249–272). Washington, DC: U.S. Department of Education.

Gottlieb, M. (1999). Assessing ESOL adolescents: Balancing accessibility to learn with accountability for learning. In C. Faltis & P. Wolfe (Eds.), *So much to say: Adolescents, bilingualism, and ESL in the secondary school* (pp. 176–204). New York: Teachers College Press.

Graves, D. (2002). *When testing lowers standards, it becomes a threat, not a tool.* Community Commentary, Monday, January 7, 2002, CELT list.

Haley, M., & Austin, T. (2004). *Content-based second language teaching and learning.* Boston, MA: Allyn & Bacon.

Harklau, L. (1994). Tracking and linguistic minority students: Consequences of ability grouping for second language learners. *Linguistics and Education, 6*(1), 221–248.

Harcourt Brace. (2003). *The Stanford English language proficiency test.* San Antonio, TX: Harcourt Educational Measurement.

McGroarty, M. (1987). Language assessment scales. In C. J. Alderson, K. J. Krahnke, & C. W. Stansfield (Eds.), *Reviews of English language proficiency tests* (pp. 51–53). Washington, DC: TESOL.

MacSwan, J. (2000). The threshold hypothesis, semilingualism, and other contributions to a deficit view of linguistic minorities. *Hispanic Journal of Behavioral Sciences, 22*(1), 3–45.

Menken, K. (2000). *What are the critical issues in wide-scale assessment of English language learners?* Retrieved May 12, 2006 from http://www.ncela.gwu.edu/pubs/tasynthesis/framing/3criticalissues.pdf

Molera, J. (2001). *Guidance regarding the implementation of A.R.S. § 15–751–755 and the Flores Consent Order.* Phoenix, AZ: Arizona Department of Education.

O'Malley, M., & Pierce, L. (1996). *Authentic assessment for English language learners: Practical Approaches for Teachers.* New York: Addison-Wesley.

Ovando, C., Collier, V., & Combs, M. C. (2003). *Bilingual & ESL classrooms: Teaching in multicultural contexts* (3rd ed.). Boston, MA: McGraw Hill.

Rumberger, R. (2004). Why students drop out. In G. Orfield (Ed.), *Dropouts in America: Confronting the graduation rate crisis* (pp. 131–156). Cambridge, MA: Harvard University Press.

Samway, K. D., & McKeon, D. (1999). *Myths and realities: Best practices for language minority students.* Portsmouth, NH: Heinemann.

Teachers of English to Speakers of Other Languages. (1997). *ESL standards for pre-K–12 students.* Alexandria, VA: Author.

Wiggins, G. (1992). Creating tests worth taking. *Educational Leadership, 26*, 26–33.

Wrigley, P. (2001). *The help! kit: A resource guide for secondary teachers of migrant English language learners.* Escort, NY: State University of New York at Oneonta.

Afterword

Anthony Magnacca/Merrill

After finishing the first eight chapters, you should be prepared to teach and assess English learners and immigrants in your classes. However, there is still much to learn that goes beyond teaching and assessing adolescent English learners. Here we offer some final thoughts about making schools more inviting to English learners and immigrant students.

Make no mistake about it, adolescent immigrant students are the fastest growing student population nationwide, entering secondary school levels at a rate nearly double that of immigrant students in elementary schools (Fix & Passell, 2003). When these students show up in school, many continue to need English instruction and support for content learning in coursework required for high school graduation, but as we have tried to show throughout this book, learning English alone is not enough to keep them in school and ensure their academic success. Multiple contextual factors contribute to school success and failure for immigrant students who are learning English; two of most salient are social relations and academic problems resulting from poverty, living in segregated neighbors, and attending segregated schools (Kozol, 2005; Rumberger, 2004). Here we focus on social relations, with an understanding that poverty and segregation need attention that goes beyond what this book has to offer.

As we have argued, successful teaching with commitments in practice is geared toward the integration of adolescent English learners into the cultural ways of learning, behaving, and using oral and written language within the various academic content areas. One of the goals of this kind of teaching is to help English learners create new identities in which they affiliate with members of established academic communities of practice.

At first glance, what we advocate may resemble to some a process of assimilation, where students first acculturate, by adopting the cultural patterns of the school, and then assimilate fully into the school culture by taking on new identities. This view follows Gordon's (1964) model of assimilation as a two-phase process. For him, assimilation starts with acculturation, where students adopt new cultural behaviors. The next phase is gaining access to the "social cliques, clubs, and institutions" of the new group. Once students gain access to and participate in these social cliques, clubs, and institutions, they can reach full assimilation (Gordon, 1964, p. 80). From this perspective, full assimilation into the school culture depends on the extent to which the school culture relinquishes its hold on the cliques, clubs, and institutions (e.g.,

AP classes, higher tracks in math and science, student council) and opens them up to newcomers it deems sufficiently acculturated.

Gordon's conceptualization of assimilation is reflected in the way many secondary schools treat immigrant students and English learners, who are expected to adopt the cultural ways of the school (learn English well; take assigned, often lower track classes; dress and talk in certain ways) *before* they can gain access to the cliques, clubs, and institutions that are afforded to students of the dominant group. Once these structural boundaries are overcome, the students can expect to be fully assimilated into the dominant group.

This conceptualization places acceptance by the dominant group at the *end* of the process, and it implies that full assimilation is the goal. We argue instead that acceptance has to happen at the *beginning* of the process of integration into the school culture, from the day a new English learner or immigrant student sets foot on campus. Moreover, we argue that full assimilation into the mainstream should not be a necessary goal. Rather, the goal should be to enable English learners and immigrant students to keep their identities and cultural affiliations while they add on new ones, especially identities and affiliations with academic communities of practice. From this perspective, assimilation is additive, in the sense that students are gaining new ways of thinking, believing, interacting, and acting without necessarily relinquishing their ethnic, language, and cultural memberships.

REDUCING SOCIAL DISTANCE AT THE OUTSET

Our position about the importance of the initial contact between English learners and the secondary school culture draws from the work of Shibutani and Kwan (1965), who theorize that how people are treated in societal institutions (including school) depends not on who they are, but on how the society defines them initially. People place other people who are outside their primary group into categories and rankings, associating them with expected behaviors and treating them accordingly. The extent to which people are defined as similar or different gives rise to the creation of *social distance*, which Shibutani and Kwan (1965) refer to as the subjective state of nearness between individuals in the dominant and new group. When social distance is low, people perceive the other as having a common identity and many shared experiences, and thus treat them as equals, making the cliques, clubs, and institutions available to them. But when social distance is high, there is a feeling that the other belongs to a different category and rank and thus requires a different treatment (Alba & Nee, 1997). When the treatment denies the other access to the cliques, clubs, and institutions of the dominant group, the other either works to overcome the discrimination and eventually gain entry or becomes a member of another group that rejects the value of the cliques, clubs, and institutions of the dominant group.

A concrete example may help here. Social distance between African American and White students has remained high despite 50 years of desegregation efforts to physically and socially integrate previously segregated schools (Kozol, 2005). One of the reasons integration has failed is because many schools have maintained a system of stratification based on perceptions of race, cultural patterns, and stereotypes to determine differential access to opportunity structures. Although individual African American students can and do succeed within this system of stratification, when a perception of high social distance between African Americans and Whites persists, and a corresponding system of stratification remains in place, success at the group level remains elusive. Some schools have been able to change perceptions and reduce social distance between African American and White students by introducing intergroup education strategies across all grade levels (Schofield, 1995; Pettigrew, 2003; Stephan & Stephan, 2003). But, by and large, perceptions of difference in abilities coupled with efforts to resegregate schools continue to contribute to high social distance between African American and White students in many school settings.

In many secondary schools, the social distance between the school and English learners is often great (Olsen, 1997; Flores-González, 2002; Gibson, Gándara, & Koyama, 2004). In these schools, teachers, peers, and school administrators tend to perceive and define adolescent newcomers and English learners as outsiders (aliens) who lower the school standards because of their low proficiency in oral and written English. When English learners and immigrant students are defined in this way, the risk for these students of developing peer group identities in opposition to the school culture is quite high (Flores-González, 2002; Hurd, 2004; Ogbu, 1978). Once this happens, it becomes increasingly difficult to convince students that the peer groups to which they belong are detrimental to their success in school (Hurd, 2004).

DON'T ACCEPT THE WAY THINGS ARE

The whole school needs to be involved in changing the system of social stratification that gives low priority to the social and academic needs of immigrant students and English learners. Systems of social stratification in school break down when teachers take a strong stance to include English learners and immigrants in all aspects of school life; when teachers view these students as capable, intelligent human beings; and when students refuse to accept unchallenging, lower track classes. As students become more aware of their worth as learners, what had once been accepted as "natural" becomes unacceptable (Shibutani & Kwan, 1965, cited in Alba & Nee, 1997, p. 836). When the school environment welcomes immigrant students and English learners, the message to these students is that the school values them. Students who feel valued are more likely to participate in school culture and less likely to engage in risky behavior by affiliating with groups who oppose school (Lewis-Charp, Yu, & Friedlaender, 2004). At first glance, it seems obvious that when students sense that they belong because the school values them, they will function better and participate more in the school culture. But, in fact, many secondary schools are not set up to welcome English learners and immigrant students (see Chapter 3), and few schools make concerted efforts to help these students fit in and feel comfortable in school (Gibson, Gándara, & Koyama, 2004). Moreover, as we pointed out above, secondary schools typically operate on the principle that acceptance of newcomers happens last, after the doors to its cherished cliques, clubs, and institutions have been opened, and these students begin to contribute in ways that are recognized and valued by the dominant group.

MAKE SCHOOLS INVITING

From our perspective, secondary schools need to provide immigrant students and English learners access to cliques, clubs, and institutions from day one. For immigrant students who are new to English and American schools, this can happen in newcomer centers and programs, as we pointed out in Chapter 3. However, there needs to be a grand scheme for ensuring that English learners feel they belong to the school. The commitments in practice do that for teaching and learning in classroom settings. Here are some ways suggested by

Gándara and Gibson (2004) to make schools inviting places for immigrant students and English learners:

- Provide newcomers and English learners with organized peer group activities both inside and outside the classroom through clubs and sports, community service activities, school improvement projects, and murals.

- Create well-structured collaborative learning groups that emphasize equal status and equal contribution. Use cross-age mentoring, pairing older and younger students to engage in school activities together.

- In large high schools, look for ways to organize students into smaller communities where students work and learn together for several years. In this way, teachers and peers get to know each student personally.

- Organize your classes and the school in ways that promote and enable students to cross ethnic, language, and socioeconomic boundaries. At the same time, help all students understand how ethnic and cultural differences can separate students, often marginalizing and alienating them from others.

- Make sure that immigrant students and English learners know who their academic counselors are and the kinds of support counselors offer for higher education.

- Create safe places, such as clubs, on the school campus for students of the same ethnic background to socialize and affirm their ethnic identities while at the same time engaging in school-related objectives.

- Offer professional development to teachers and administrators on teaching immigrant students and English learners as well as on intergroup education programs.

These suggestions require investments into secondary schools that go beyond the commitments in practice teachers need to work effectively with immigrant students and English learners. Quite simply, the effective use of the commitments in practice that we advocate and present in this book is connected to how immigrant students and English learners are perceived and defined when they enter school. We urge you to make your secondary school as inviting and open to immigrant students and English learners as it is for youth who come to school already proficient in oral and written English.

References

Alba, R., & Nee, V. (1997). Rethinking assimilation theory for a new era of immigration. *International Migration Review, 31*(4), 826–874.

Fix, J., & Passell, M. (2003). *U.S. immigration: Trends and implications for schools.* Retrieved June 10, 2006, from http://www.urban.org/url.cfm?ID=410644

Flores-González, N. (2002). *School kids/street kids: Identity development in Latino students.* New York: Teachers College Press.

Gándara, P., & Gibson, M. (2004). Peers and school performance: Implications for research, policy, and practice. In M. Gibson, P. Gándara, & J. P. Koyama (Eds.), *School connections: U.S. Mexican youth, peers, and school achievement* (pp. 173–192). New York: Teachers College Press.

Gibson, M., Gándara, P., & Koyama, J. (2004). *School connections: U.S. Mexican youth, peers, and school achievement.* New York: Teachers College Press.

Gordon, M. (1964). *Assimilation in American life.* New York: Oxford University Press.

Hurd, C. (2004). "Acting out" and being a "schoolboy": Performance in an ELD classroom. In M. Gibson, P. Gándara, & J. P. Koyama (Eds.), *School connections: U.S. Mexican youth, peers, and school achievement* (pp. 63–86). New York: Teachers College Press.

Kozol, J. (2005). *The shame of the nation: The restoring of apartheid schooling in America.* New York: Crown Publishers.

Lewis-Charp, H., Yu, H. C., & Friedlaender, D. (2004). The influence of intergroup relations on school engagement: Two cases. In M. Gibson, P. Gándara, & J. P. Koyama (Eds.), *School connections: U.S. Mexican youth, peers, and school achievement* (pp. 107–128). New York: Teachers College Press.

Ogbu, J. (1978). *Minority education and caste: The American system in cross-cultural perspective.* New York: Academic Press.

Olsen, L. (1997). *Made in America: Immigrant students in our public schools.* New York: The New Press.

Pettigrew, T. (2003). Intergroup contact: Theory, research, and new perspectives. In J. Banks & C. McGee Banks (Eds.), *Handbook of research on multicultural education* (2nd ed., pp. 770–781). San Francisco: Jossey-Bass.

Rumberger, R. (2004). Why students drop out. In G. Orfield (Ed.), *Dropouts in America: Confronting the graduation crisis* (pp. 131–156). Cambridge, MA: Harvard Education Press.

Schofield, J. (1995). Improving intergroup relations among students. In J. Banks & C. M. Banks (Eds.), *Handbook of research on multicultural education* (pp. 635–646). New York: Macmillan.

Shibutani, T., & Kwan, K. (1965). *Ethnic stratification.* New York: Macmillan.

Stephan, W., & Stephan, C. W. (2003). Intergroup relations in multicultural education programs. In J. Banks & C. McGee Banks (Eds.), *Handbook of research on multicultural education* (2nd ed., pp. 782–798). San Francisco: Jossey-Bass.

Index